The Words and the Music and the Tears that Fell

By Tracy Dartt and Forrest Dartt

With Sharon Dartt, Don Dartt, and BJ Speer

Tracy Dartt and Forrest Dartt

Table of Contents

Foreword

Tracy Dartt spent a lifetime writing, singing, recording, and pitching the songs God gave him. He had a natural talent to take truths from the scriptures and express them with a minimal amount of words, often from a unique viewpoint that would bring the listener to an Aha! moment. He wrote many songs about Heaven, and looking forward to meeting the Savior face to face, as well as catching up with those friends and loved ones who have gone on before. He wrote funny songs that made us "church folk" take a long, hard look in the mirror to analyze whether some of our methods border on the ridiculous. The Dartts were not limited to any certain style or genre of music when they recorded Tracy's tunes, and a wide variety of influences is evident in their repertoire.

Tracy left a lot more than songs behind when he took his Heavenly flight on April 7, 2022. He left a legacy of loving the Lord, loving the souls of others, and a reputation of living the truths that he sang and preached. His life was full of mountains and valleys, and Tracy was faithful to trust God and seek His will through it all. Though we miss his deep baritone voice and his keen wit and wisdom, he had become more of a Godly man than this world could contain any longer.

Please enjoy this collection of songs that originally appeared on the Kindle Vella platform in the form of episodes. The lyrics, the scripture references, and the memoirs combine to make a useful daily devotional book. Most of the songs and their soundtracks can be downloaded from online music services, while others can be enjoyed on youtube.com for free. Please enjoy them, share them, and even sing them with anyone who will listen and be blessed.

Forrest Dartt, founding member of the Dartts gospel quartet, and middle son of Tracy and Sharon Dartt

Preface

I had a desire to write a book using the songs I had written, and the stories behind them. The original plan was to keep the stories short, and include scriptures to support the lyrics. I have always felt that it is of utmost importance to make sure that what I had written is true to Biblical principles. Our prayer is that these writings will be a blessing to many people. The songs can also be heard on many streaming services, such as Apple music, Spotify, and Youtube. I hope you enjoy the book, and Lord willing, we will do our best to continue with subsequent volumes...

-Dr. Tracy Dartt, author of 'God on the Mountain' and many other original gospel songs, and Patriarch of the musical Dartt family.

Dad did not live long enough to see this second book come to pass. Many of the family members pitched in a song or two to help complete the number of episodes required to publish it. Sharon, Don, BJ Speer, and myself (Forrest) contributed episodes to go along with songs we had written and recorded, and I made several more episodes out of Dad's songs after he passed. This book is for him, but more importantly, its aim is to extend the reach of his love for your soul, his beautiful artistry, and his witness for Christ beyond the active ministry of the Dartts and the years of Tracy's life here on Earth.

-Forrest Dartt, founding member of the Dartts gospel quartet, and middle son of Tracy and Sharon Dartt

Today

Over, and over, and over again,

Jesus has asked you to let Him come in.

He loves you and He'll take away all your sin,

But time after time, you've turned Him away.

Over, and over, you've known deep inside,

Your need for salvation just won't be denied.

The only thing holding you back is your pride,

But time and again, you've turned Him away

Chorus:

Today is the day of salvation, now is the time

You know you must be born again.

Jesus has made the provision, He gave His life,

That through Him you might be saved.

God, in His mercy, is calling again

There's just no need to be bound in your sin.

Tracy Dartt and Forrest Dartt

Today is the day your new life can begin.

Today is the day of salvation.

Over, and over, and over again,

Jesus has asked you to let Him come in.

He loves you and He'll take away all your sin.

Don't miss this chance today.

Words and Music by Tracy G. Dartt   Copyright 1979

Today

Today, I find myself knocking at the door of the scheduling nurse, to set a date for my upcoming spinal surgery. It's been three days, and no answer. I've called and left three messages; but no answer. What am I supposed to do now? How can I know the next steps I need to take until this is resolved? I will try again tomorrow, because my life is on hold until I get an answer.

There are times that the Lord knocks on our heart's door, and we fail to answer. Sometimes, we just put it off, or even ignore it altogether. Whatever His calling may be; for our salvation, for surrendering ourselves to Him and His service, or for a commitment of some kind. We need to realize that there will be consequences to pay for ignoring God's call to come to Him. We cannot be effective

Christians if we do not respond when God knocks on the doors of our hearts and lives. What is it in your life that is keeping you from responding to God's personal invitation? He can forgive your sin. He will provide everything you need. He can raise the dead. He has given all of us gifts to share.

When God called Samuel over and over again in the middle of the night, Eli, the High Priest, told him to answer, "Speak Lord, for thy servant hearth." When Samuel spoke those words in response to God's calling, God gave him a message that would change not only his life, but the entire nation of Israel, affecting many generations of God's children to come.

There is love, joy, peace, and protection in the center of His will. Seek it. God has a plan for your life. Sometimes we pray and ask Him to come and be about our business, instead of asking Him how we can be about His business. Why not take the first step today? Respond to God's call, and He will guide your next steps.

Revelation 3:20   Behold, I stand at the door, and knock: if any man hear my voice, and open the door, I will come in to him, and will sup with him, and he with me.

Psalms 143:10-12   Teach me to do thy will; for thou art my God: thy spirit is good; lead me into the land of uprightness. Quicken me, O LORD, for thy name's sake: for thy righteousness' sake bring my soul out of trouble. And of thy mercy cut off mine enemies, and destroy all them that afflict my soul: for I am thy servant.

The original recording of this song is available for download (just search "Tracy Dartt Today") from the following music subscription services: Amazon Music, Apple Music, iTunes, Spotify, and Youtube Music.

Tracy Dartt and Forrest Dartt

Take a Look at Yourself

Take a look at yourself, do you like what you see?

Is everything just like you want it to be?

Or are you anxious and so afraid,

'Cause you know you need some changes made?

Take a look at yourself, do you like what you find?

Is there happiness there, and peace of mind?

Or does fear and darkness surround your day,

Are you searching hard, tryin' to find your way?

Chorus:

Look in the mirror of God's Word.

Don't you remember the things you've heard?

Not just a hearer, but a doer, too,

Won't you do the things Jesus asks you to do?

God's Word is a mirror to your soul,

That you may know who's in control.

The Words and the Music and the Tears that Fell

And by the Spirit of the Lord,

You'll be changed to His image from glory to glory.

Take a look at yourself, do you like what you see?

Is everything just like you want it to be?

In the things you do and the things you say,

Are you growing more like Him every day?

Take a look at yourself. Take a look at yourself.

Take a look at yourself.

Words & Music by Tracy G. Dartt   Copyright 1979

Take a Look at Yourself

As a boy, I remember that we took New Year's Eve and New Year's Day as an opportunity for personal examination and improvement. It was all about a new start, a new beginning. Everyone was encouraged to make a list of "New Year's Resolutions." In high school, we would ask each other about our resolutions. It was usually about being a better person. A lot of people would commit to losing weight or quitting smoking, overcoming a bad habit, keeping a promise, or being a true friend. These things are not just for young people, adults need to consider these same commitments. Keeping our resolutions is not easy. Sometimes, it's very difficult and takes some extreme effort.

Have you ever looked in a mirror and been surprised or disappointed in your appearance? In my own imagination, I look like a superstar, but that isn't what everyone else sees. When I get in front of the mirror, I am reminded that I have work to do. The standard for the Christian to measure character and conduct is the Word of God. *James 1:23-24* says this: *"For if any be a hearer of the word, and not a doer, he is like unto a man beholding his natural face in a glass: for he beholdeth himself, and goeth his way, and straightway forgetteth what manner of man he was."* When we take a look at ourselves in God's mirror, we need to ask for His help to stick to our resolutions, so when other people see us, we will be a reflection of God's love toward them.

When Peter heard the rooster crow after he denied Jesus for the third time, he was reminded of his own failure to measure up to the resolution of pledging his love and loyalty to Christ. What commitments have you made? The scriptures tell us, as Christians, we need to examine ourselves, whether we be "in" the faith. When we fail to measure up to the standard, we must practice being doers of the Word, and not just hearers. Let us resolve to be better Christians, seeking God's will, and living up to it.

II Corinthians 3:18   But we all, with open face beholding as in a glass the glory of the Lord, are changed into the same image from glory to glory, even as by the Spirit of the Lord.

This song is available for download (just search "Tracy Dartt take a look at yourself") from the following music subscription services: Amazon Music, Apple Music, iTunes, Spotify, and Youtube Music.

He Gave Me Mercy

He gave me strength in my moment of weakness.

He gave me hope, when hope was gone.

And He gave me joy, when sorrow had bowed me to despair,

And when I deserved judgement, He gave me mercy.

Chorus:

I don't understand how anyone could love me this way.

I don't understand why He paid the price He had to pay.

For I am not worthy that He should want to give His life for me.

But when I deserved judgement, He gave me mercy.

He gave me peace in the midst of my trials.

He gave me life, though it cost His own.

And He gave me love, when loved ones

and friends had turned away

And when I deserved judgement, He gave me mercy.

Words and Music by Tracy G. Dartt   Copyright 1981

He Gave Me Mercy

"When I deserved justice, He gave me mercy." I wrote this little song after having two incidents take place in the same day, where mercy was cast aside by the letter of the law. We had paid a tax bill on time, but it was returned to us because of a technicality. Then, later that same day, one of our sons was given a speeding ticket, for a speed that he could not possibly have attained in this particular circumstance. Mercy was not shown in either instance.

Noah Webster, in his dictionary, published in the year 1828, defines the word mercy as the following: "that benevolence, mildness, or tenderness of heart which disposes a person to overlook injuries or treat an offender better than he deserves."

In Jesus's telling of the parable of the lost son (Luke 15:11-32), He gives us a great illustration of mercy and forgiveness. The younger of two sons came to his father and asked him for his portion of his inheritance. The father divided the inheritance to both of his sons. The younger son took his portion and went off to a far country. There, he wasted everything on "riotous living." The young man ended up working in the fields, feeding swine. He had fallen about as low as he could go, because the pig is considered to be an unclean animal by the Jews. Then, the story goes on to say, he came to himself. He realized what he had become. He said, "My father's hired servants are better off than me. I will arise and go to my father and say unto him, Father, I have sinned against Heaven and before thee, and am no more worthy to be called thy son. Make me as one of thy servants." The son came in repentance. His father gave him mercy, instead of the judgement he deserved. He welcomed him home and said to his servants, "Bring forth the best robe and put it on him, and put a ring on his hand, and shoes on his feet. And bring forth hither the fatted calf and kill it, and let us eat and be merry. For this my son was dead and is alive again, he was lost and is found." And they began to be merry! What a wonderful picture of salvation!!

The Words and the Music and the Tears that Fell

Our God is a God of love, mercy, and forgiveness, no matter what the circumstance. Those who serve Him and keep His covenant and His testimonies are treated according to grace and mercy, and not judgment according to the letter of the law.

Psalms 32:10   Many sorrows shall be to the wicked: but he that trusteth in the Lord, mercy shall compass him about.

Lamentations 3:22-23   It is of the Lord's mercies that we are not consumed, because His compassions fail not. They are new every morning: great is thy faithfulness.

Psalms 103:17-18   But the mercy of the Lord is from everlasting to everlasting upon them that fear Him, and His righteousness unto children's children; To such as keep His covenant, and to those that remember His commandments to do them.

This song is available to stream (just search "Tracy Dartt He gave me mercy") on Youtube.com

Tracy Dartt and Forrest Dartt

Country Congregation

Rolling down a dusty, country highway

Glory in the Sunday morning sun

I see the white crowned steeple rise before me

I hear the morning singing has begun

It's the country congregation

They believe in soul's salvation

They're the backbone of the nation

Little country congregation

Something about the singin' that excites you

You know that it is coming from their heart

And such a friendly spirit that invites you

You know somehow you must become a part

Of the country congregation

They believe in soul's salvation

The Words and the Music and the Tears that Fell

They're the backbone of the nation

Little country congregation

Words and Music by Tracy G. Dartt   Copyright 1975

Country Congregation

When we moved to our country house in Tennessee, we were blessed to find a "Country Congregation." It's a wonderful little church, only about one tenth of a mile from our house. We were welcomed there with open arms by a loving, caring assembly of believers. Only the choir could be heard singing on the fellowship hymn, everyone else was busy greeting and hugging one another! It was delightful!

The local church assembly is so important to the life of the believer. People pray for each other's needs, and often sacrifice to help each other. They sing together the songs of praise and joy. They hear the preaching and teaching of God's Word. They are encouraged to seek God's will and to find the ministry that He has for their lives. They are encouraged to share their faith with those around them. They are taught to bring their tithes and offerings to the Lord, that He might bless them in return. Thank the Lord for the local church!

Over all the years of our traveling music ministry, we have sung in hundreds of churches of all sizes. We sang for audiences of 3,000 to 4,000 and for as few as 5. The size of the church does not really matter. It is the presence of the Spirit of God that counts. It just so happens that often the smaller churches, with an attendance of 200 or less, often develop a really friendly and welcoming spirit.

When I sang with The Victors Quartet in the late 1960's, I scheduled the group to sing in a little mission church in Tecate, Mexico. We drove around the town the night before the concert. There was a lot of poverty in evidence. We saw people that looked like they were starving, and children bloated with hunger. The next day, the pastor and his family prepared a meal for us after the Sunday morning concert. The meal consisted of baloney sandwiches, made with fresh tomatoes and onions. It was delicious!

We sat in the church auditorium, resting after lunch. Our piano player went outside to look around the property and he came back with a sad look on his face. He said, "The pastor and his family haven't eaten. They gave us their food." We were all saddened to hear that. We prayed for them and dug up the cash we had between us. It came to about $72.00, and we gave it to them for an offering. We hoped and prayed that we would be able to buy fuel with a credit card on the way home. They sacrificed for us, we could not leave without giving back to them.

Hebrews 10:23-25   Let us hold fast the profession of our faith without wavering; (for He is faithful that promised;) And let us consider one another to provoke unto love and to good works: Not forsaking the assembling of ourselves together, as the manner of some is; but exhorting one another: and so much the more, as ye see the day approaching.

This song is available to stream (just search "Country Congregation by June Wade and the Country Congregation") on Youtube.com

Think On These

Oh, you know from time to time, the devil preys upon your mind

And he tempts you with the thoughts that lead to sin.

Do not yield unto temptation, for the God of your salvation

Will deliver you and give you peace within.

Chorus:

Whatsoever things are true, whatsoever things are honest,

The just, the pure and lovely things there be,

If there be any good, if there be any virtue,

If there be any praise, then think on these.

Oh. you know from day to day, Old Satan tries to block your way,

And those thoughts that lead to trouble cross your mind.

Do not keep those thoughts within, for they just might turn to sin.

Just think about the good things that you'll find.

Words and Music by Tracy G. Dartt   Copyright 1972

Think On These

Dr. Norman Vincent Peale wrote his famous book, "The Power of Positive Thinking". I wrote a sermon once, entitled "The Positive of Powerful Thinking". Dr. Peale's emphasis was on thinking positively and avoiding the negative. My sermon was about realizing the unlimited power that is ours through prayer as a child of God. *Proverbs 23:7* says *"As a man thinketh in his heart, so is he."* One of the most difficult things in life to control is our thought life. "The secret you inside" is a phrase from one of my songs. Our thoughts are not secret at all. *Psalms 94:11" The LORD knoweth the thoughts of man, that they are vanity."*

We see many times in the in the New Testament that as Jesus was dealing with people, He knew their thoughts. As Jesus was choosing the men who would be His disciples, He chose a man by the name of Philip. Philip then found his friend, Nathaniel, and told him, "We have found him whom Moses, in the law and the prophets did write, Jesus of Nazareth, the son of Joseph." Then when Jesus saw Nathaniel coming toward Him, He said to him, "Behold, an Israelite indeed, in whom is no guile." Nathaniel was amazed when he was told by Jesus that he had been seen when he was under the fig tree, and that Jesus had known his thoughts. Nathaniel answered Jesus and said, "Rabbi, thou art the Son of God; thou art the King of Israel.'"

As it has been revealed to us that God knows our thoughts and the desires of our hearts, let us endeavor to think on the things that are good. Let us read, study and memorize the Word of God. Psalms 119:11 tells us that when we hide God's Word in our hearts, it will keep us from sinning against God. Listening to good Christ-centered music helps to keep our minds and hearts focused on the things of God. Paul, the apostle, wrote to the church in Thessalonica: *"Pray without ceasing. In everything give thanks: for this is the will of God in Christ Jesus concerning you."* Let us seek the Lord and His will for our lives. Think on these things.

II Corinthians 10:5   Casting down imaginations, and every high thing that exalteth itself against the knowledge of God, and bringing into captivity every thought to the obedience of Christ.

Philippians 4:8-9   Finally, brethren, whatsoever things are true, whatsoever things are honest, whatsoever things are just, whatsoever things are pure, whatsoever things are lovely, whatsoever things are of good report; if there be any virtue, and if there be any praise, think on these things.

Hebrews 4:12-13   For the word of God is quick, and powerful, and sharper than any two-edged sword, piercing even to the dividing asunder of soul and spirit, and of the joints and marrow, and is a discerner of the thoughts and intents of the heart.

This song is available to stream (just search "Listen for the sound of the Weatherford Quartet LP") on Youtube.com. Click "Show more" on the left side of the page above the comments to see the playlist. "Think on These" is song #2, and it starts at 1:29 on the timeline. Tracy is singing bass on this recording by the Weatherford Quartet.

Tracy Dartt and Forrest Dartt

Let's Take Time

Sometimes we take the time to sort

the good times from the bad times.

We separate the bitter from the sweet.

We like to remember all the things that made us happy

And forget the things that brought us to defeat.

But remember that the bad times

may have brought about the good times,

And in every life a little rain must fall.

So sometimes when things are bad, take a look at what you have,

And they may not be such bad times, after all.

Chorus:

So let's take time to be thankful for the good times.

Count your blessings, and be thankful every day.

When things go wrong, they're just bound to get better,

So get ready for some good to come your way.

The Words and the Music and the Tears that Fell

Sometimes we fret and worry

about what may come tomorrow,

As if things weren't bad enough today.

But I don't believe that life

would be so full of tears and sorrow,

If we'd take some time to smile along the way.

For they say in back of every cloud

there is a silver lining,

And a rainbow follows every stormy sky.

To be sad is no disgrace,

but a smile upon your face

Will make the world seem brighter by and by.

Words and Music by Tracy G. Dartt   Copyright 1974

Let's Take Time

"We go through the present blindfolded...only later, when the blindfold is removed, and we examine the past, do we realize what we've been through and understand what it means." Milan Kundara

25

Oh, how many times through the years have I wondered why I was going through a certain trial or situation. Then later, I would look back and see that it was God's way, of preparing me for something really good. We have to experience some of life's unpleasantries to be ready to fulfill God's will. Often, it is to prepare us to minister to the needs of others."

We were just finishing up a five month tour of our solo ministry. In those solo years, we traveled with our whole family. My wife, Sharon, our sons, Don, Frosty, and Stoney, and our daughter, Peachy. Just one more booking and it was a big one at Camp Chataqua in Ohio, right next to the Great Miami River. We were supposed to sing every night for a week for the Michigan Fellowship of Bible Baptist Churches. It was a great opportunity to meet with leaders of several new churches, for our ministry.

As we drove the bus through the gate, we were met by the camp director. He informed us that the Michigan people called, and had to cancel. They had tried to reach us but were unable to. No cell phones in those days. He said, "Sorry, Brother Dartt! You can stay here if you like, you'll be here all alone, but the whole facility is yours. Help yourself to whatever, we'll be back in a week." He handed me the keys and drove away with his family. There we were, alone at Camp Chataqua. No offerings, no music sales, no expense check, and too late to rebook anything else. What do we do now?

We said, "Hey! We're tired! Let's just rest and enjoy it." We checked out the facilities - not bad! We had a comfortable cabin, tennis courts, shuffleboard, a swimming pool, and even an electric golf cart to drive around the camp. We had plenty of food on the bus, and we even had permission to empty the ice cream and soda dispensers. All in all, the whole family had a blast! Not such a bad time after all!

Romans 8:28   And we know that all things work together for good to them that love God, to them who are the called according to His purpose.

Philippians 4:4   Rejoice in the Lord alway: and again I say, Rejoice.

I Thessalonians 5:18   In every thing give thanks: for this is the will of God in Christ Jesus concerning you.

Look up The Dartts and Tracy Dartt on most music subscription services to find many of the songs featured in these episodes. This song can be found on Youtube.com, just search: "Let's take time song masters" in the search bar

Tracy Dartt and Forrest Dartt

God On The Mountain Part II

Life is easy when you're up on the mountain,

And you've got peace of mind like you've never known.

But when things change and you're down in the valley

Don't lose faith for you're never alone.

Chorus:

The God on the mountain is still God in the valley.

When things go wrong He'll make them right.

And the God of the good times is still God in the bad times.

The God of the day is still God in the night.

We talk of faith when we're up on that mountain,

But talk comes easy when life's at it's best.

But in the valley of trials and temptations,

That's when faith is really put to the test.

Words and Music by Tracy G. Dartt   Copyright 1974

God On The Mountain Part II

In 1974 we moved from Oklahoma back to California. I bought into a swimming pool business with my friend, Joe, in Victorville. My partner and I seemed to be doing very well. I was selling the pools, and Joe built the pools. Our bookkeeper kept telling us that we were making too much money, and that we needed to invest more back into the company. We bought a truck, a ditch witch (digger), and extra pool equipment. It seemed almost too good to be true! As it turned out, it was too good to be true. As the building season began to come to a close, I noticed something was wrong. I spoke to my partner, and told him that our bank accounts were dwindling too quickly, and that we would not be able to finish all the pools that were under construction. I spent a weekend going over the books and discovered that we were losing an average of $500 per pool. After consulting with the bookkeeper, he realized that he had been using the wrong bookkeeping method. My partner wanted to declare bankruptcy, but I said that it would not be right to do that. He invited me to take the company over, and signed the business over to me.

My wife and I prayed about it and God answered. I kept selling pools, even in the off season. We eventually lost the pool business, but all the pools were able to be finished. Praise the Lord, we didn't have to bankrupt. It was while we were going through this struggle that I wrote The God On The Mountain. I woke up in the middle of the night and wrote two songs, "The God On The Mountain" and "Sing Me An Old Gospel Song." The words just seemed to flow and both songs were finished in about 30 minutes, and I went back to sleep. It was as if The God On The Mountain was a special message to me. God was letting me know that He would see us through this trial.

This song was recorded for the first time in 1975, while my wife, Sharon, and I were singing with The Country Congregation. God used a friend of mine, who owned Calvary Records, to provide the opportunity to record. The God On The Mountain was one of 9 songs that I wrote for the project, In 1988 a group called The McKameys from Tennessee recorded the song. There was some hesitation about recording it, but without it they didn't have enough songs for their album. It was a big hit for them. It was this version of the song that became #1 on the southern gospel charts, and sold over 200,000 albums.

Years later, Bill Gaither sent the song to Lynda Randle, but she felt that it was too country for her. Her husband convinced her to focus on the lyrics, and give the song another chance. It was a huge hit for Lynda, and still is!

Unexpected good news arrived today, as I began to write The God On The Mountain Part II. My wife received a text from a friend in Texas, telling her that her husband had purchased 100 new hymnals for their church. As they thumbed through the pages, they found that The God On The Mountain was one of the songs included in the book. It is amazing how God has blessed this song! It was #1 in the southern gospel charts in the United States for 5 months, and remained in the chart for 2 years. It has been used in over 60 countries, translated into at least 8 languages, and recorded well over 200 times.

What does it feel like to have written such a popular song? Simply stated, I feel very blessed and humbled. It was the Lord's doing - nothing I could have done myself. God put me in the right place, at the right time, and in the right circumstances.

The reason so many people can relate to this song, is that it helps us relate our circumstances, our lives, our hopes and fears to God in a very personal way. God's love goes way beyond the mountains and the valleys, the good times and the bad times, the day and the night. He is the God of the people, and we, His people want to sing about

Him and praise His name! Can you imagine how it makes God feel, when He hears us sing this song and worship him? Remember, He has given us everything we have, and we can never give back more than He has given us.

This song, and its soundtrack (if you want to use it to perform the song yourself) is available for download (just search "The Dartts God on the Mountain") from the following music subscription services: Amazon Music, Apple Music, iTunes, Spotify, and Youtube Music

Tracy Dartt and Forrest Dartt

God Has Given Me The Victory

Traveling along life's lonely highway,

Fettered and chained in the bonds of sin.

Trying my best to do it my way,

Having no peace, no joy within.

The devil had bowed me to destruction,

Sorrow and hell my final home,

Then I met Jesus, changed my direction,

My sins are all gone.

God has given me the victory, (Victory is mine)

And to Him belongs the glory. (Glory all divine)

For I heard an old, old story, (Heard an old, old story)

How He sent His dear Son (Sent His only Son)

To extend the invitation (Come ye unto me)

To share the gift of salvation. (Gift so full and free)

God has given me the victory, (Victory is mine)

And the battle's been won.

The Words and the Music and the Tears that Fell

Now I go on my way rejoicing,

Singing a song to Christ my King.

Trusting my life to His direction,

I have surrendered everything.

Going to join the saints in Heaven,

Knowing a mansion's waiting there.

Praise God, I met Jesus, changed my direction,

My sins are all gone.

Words and Music by Tracy G. Dartt   Copyright 1980

God Has Given Me The Victory

Jesus said in *John 3:5-6 ...Except a man be born of water and of the Spirit, he cannot enter into the kingdom of God. That which is born of the flesh is flesh; and that which is born of the Spirit is spirit.* Born of the Spirit! The new birth! Born again. When you experience this new birth, you enter into the realm of the Spirit and the Holy Spirit comes to live within you. You are brought from spiritual death to spiritual life. In this spiritual awakening, you have caused your enemy, the devil, to be aroused against you. You have entered into a warfare of the spirit, but you are not alone. The Holy Spirit within you brings you into a personal relationship with God, who will fight every battle with you. The power of God within you will enable you to overcome the attacks of the enemy.

II Corinthians 10: 3-5 tells us this: *"For though we walk in the flesh, we do not war after the flesh: (For the weapons of our warfare are not carnal [fleshly], but mighty through God to the pulling down of strongholds.) Casting down imaginations, and every high thing that exalteth itself against the knowledge of God, and bringing into captivity every thought to the obedience of Christ."* Though we do not need to fear our enemy, we do need to be expecting his attacks. And remember that we are told in *II Timothy 1:7, "For God hath not given us the spirit of fear; but of power, and of love, and of a sound mind."*

At 77 years of age, I've lived a full life. I've traveled all 50 states, and a few foreign countries. I've met thousands of people, many of whom were facing deep trials and even life threatening situations. You can quickly discern the difference between a born again Christian and a person without Christ.

The trial may be the same, but the way it is handled is strikingly different. Those without faith are most often filled with fear, anguish, doubt, and hopelessness. But the child of God, who has faith, trust, and hope, can even find gladness and joy in the face of adversity.

Hebrews 11:33-34   Who through faith subdued kingdoms, wrought righteousness, obtained promises, stopped the mouths of lions, Quenched the violence of fire, escaped the edge of the sword, out of weakness were made strong, waxed valiant in fight, turned to flight the armies of the aliens.

I Peter 5:8   Be sober, be vigilant; because your adversary the devil, as a roaring lion, walketh about, seeking whom he may devour.

The Words and the Music and the Tears that Fell

I Corinthians 15:57   But thanks be to God, which giveth us the victory through our Lord Jesus Christ.

This song is available for download (just search "Tracy Dartt God has given me the victory") from the following music subscription services: Amazon Music, Apple Music, iTunes, Spotify, and Youtube Music

Tracy Dartt and Forrest Dartt

Chances of a Lifetime

Many times, many places,

Many people, many faces,

All too soon they seem to pass

Like sand within the hour glass.

The years of time flow quickly by

So soon they even seem to fly,

And the chances of a life time soon are gone.

Chorus:

Don't let the time slip away,

Don't let each chance slip through your fingers.

There may not be another day,

And time goes on, it never lingers.

Won't you stop and count the cost?

He who hesitates is lost,

And the chances of a lifetime soon are gone.

The Words and the Music and the Tears that Fell

Many people, so many souls

Searching for their different goals.

Some for fortune, some for fame,

But in the end, they're all the same.

And when their life on earth is done,

And they stand before God's throne,

Then the chances of a lifetime will be gone.

Words and Music by Tracy G. Dartt   Copyright 1975

Chances of a Lifetime

Each day of our life is a slice of time, given to us as a gift. Each day has its chances and its opportunities. Opportunities to accomplish something, from the smallest intercessory prayer, to major life changing moments or decisions. It's up to us to wake up, arise, and redeem those moments before they are gone forever.

Some years ago, when I was working in the Los Angeles area, I was planning my vacation. I had decided to take my wife, Sharon, and our kids to my hometown, St. Paul, Minnesota to see my father. I had not seen him for several years. He had not met my wife, nor seen his grandchildren, but most important of all, we did not believe that he was saved (born again).

My dad was an alcoholic and was living on skid row. My mom and I had left him in 1959 and had moved to southern California to live with my grandmother. While attending high school there, my music teacher invited me to attend his church. He needed bass singers in the church choir. It was in that church that I first heard the gospel, and received Christ as my personal Savior. I had met my wife-to-be in the same high school, and we were married in 1964. By this time, we had a son, Donald, and a little girl, "Peachy." We were buying our first home, and we were attending a great church.

I began thinking about Dad, and praying for him, and had even begun to write a letter to him. God had blessed me with the ability to forgive him for the very difficult years he had caused for me and for my mother. The last time I had seen my dad was when I flew home to visit my older brother, just before he died of leukemia in 1962.

We made the plans and set aside the time to make the trip to Minnesota. About a month before we were scheduled to leave, I received a call from my sister-in-law. She said, "Tracy, your dad has passed away. He died in a storeroom in back of a bar, where he earned a place to sleep by sweeping up at night." There was no funeral. The state had buried him in a pauper's grave. It was a shock - my opportunity had passed - my chance was gone, never to return.

Don't let the time slip away, and make your decisions prayerfully and wisely. Is there a chance in your life that could be slipping away? Don't wait until it's too late to forgive someone who has wronged you, or to ask forgiveness of someone you have wronged.

James 4:14   Whereas ye know not what shall be on the morrow. For what is your life? It is but a vapour that appeareth for a little time and then vanisheth away."

James 1:5   If any of you lack wisdom, let him ask of God, that giveth to all men liberally, and upbraideth (reproaches) not: and it shall be given him.

This song is available for download (just search "BJ Speer chances of a lifetime") from the following music subscription services: Amazon Music, Apple Music, iTunes, Spotify, and Youtube Music

Brand New Feeling

Gone are the dreams of yesterday

Gone are the troubles that did bind me.

All of my sorrows washed away,

All of my burdens left behind me.

Chorus:

I've got a brand new feeing, brand new feeling

Brand new feeling in my soul

In my soul.

Now I have life for evermore.

No more can sin and death confine me.

And though some tears may be in store,

New life with meaning is before me.

This life is waiting now for you

The Master's knocking, let Him enter.

The Words and the Music and the Tears that Fell

His love is real, His word is true.

Make Him your friend, your Lord, your Savior

Words and Music by Tracy G. Dartt   Copyright 1969

Brand New Feeling

"Brand New Feeling" is the first song I ever wrote. At the time, I was singing bass with the Victors Quartet, a gospel group, working out of Hollywood, California. We were a part-time group, and sang in churches on the weekends. We also recorded background music for other artists. The manager and high tenor in the group was my good friend, Al Harkins. Al was a gifted writer himself, and had written several gospel songs that were popular at the time. Some of his songs were "It's In Your Hands," "Jesus Is The Bridge Over Troubled Waters," and "He Didn't Come Down." He became my mentor and encouraged me to write songs.

We were gathering material to record an album for Capitol Records. It was very exciting to be on a major label and, at the time, we were the only gospel group recording for Capitol. Our friend, Steve Stone, was the producer for Tennessee Ernie Ford, and also for our quartet, The Victors. The members of our quartet got together to choose the title song for our album, and to my surprise, they chose my song, "Brand New Feeling."

This song celebrates what happened in my own life when I accepted the fact that Jesus is the only begotten Son of Almighty God. I believed in my heart that His death on the cross was the sacrifice made for my sins. I believed that He was buried and did, indeed, raise again from the dead, as He had told His disciples He would do. When I believed these things I prayed for salvation and I was born again, and the Holy Spirit of God came to live within me. I became a new creature. I had a new beginning. Old desires changed, and I was given a new love for people that I could not love before. My dreams and goals changed. Finding the will of God and His plan for my life became foremost in my thoughts. I am not perfect, there is always a conflict between the old man and the new. However, the conflict itself is proof that there has been a change. I am so thankful that I was introduced to the truth of the gospel as a young man. I was given a brand new life, a brand new start, and a Brand New Feeling!!

2 Corinthians 5:17-18   Therefore if any man be in Christ, he is a new creature: old things are passed away; behold, all things are become new. And all things are of God, who hath reconciled us to Himself, by Jesus Christ, and hath given to us the ministry of reconciliation.

Romans 8:8-9   So they that are in the flesh cannot please God. But ye are not in the flesh, but in the Spirit, if so be that the Spirit of God dwell in you. Now if any man have not the Spirit of Christ, he is none of His.

Romans 10:9-10   That if thou shalt confess with thy mouth the Lord Jesus, and shalt believe in thine heart that God hath raised Him from the dead, thou shalt be saved. For with the heart man believeth unto righteousness; and with the mouth confession is made to salvation.

This song is available for download (just search "Don Dartt Brand New Feeling") from the following music subscription services: Amazon Music, Apple Music, iTunes, Spotify, and Youtube Music

How Far Do Your Roots Go Down?

How far do your roots go down?

Better dig deeper into the ground

The soil of the word is very sound

How far do your roots go down?

Are you satisfied to be a little sprout

Or do your branches ache to spread on out?

He's planted the seed, now it's time to proceed

And dig for the nutrients you need

How far do your roots go down?

Better dig deeper into the ground

The soil of the word is very sound

How far do your roots go down?

Don't be stuck like a stick in the mud

Or when springtime comes you'll fail to bud

Tracy Dartt and Forrest Dartt

Oh, You've got to know you can never grow

Until you place those roots below

How far do your roots go down?

Better dig deeper into the ground

The soil of the word is very sound

How far do your roots go down?

A tree planted by the living water

With roots grounded firmly in the Word

Brings fruit and shade, and in the hottest part of the day

A cool drink is brought up from the earth

Words and Music by Forrest Dartt   Copyright 2000

How Far Do Your Roots Go Down?   Forrest Dartt:

Psalm 1:3   And he shall be like a tree planted by the rivers of water, that bringeth forth his fruit in his season, His leaf also shall not wither; and whatsoever he doeth shall prosper.

I remember when I was a little guy, I would sit on the front row and watch my Dad (Tracy) sing in churches while my Mom (Sharon) played the piano. We had concerts three to four nights a week, and I heard the same songs over and over again. Fortunately, the songs my Dad wrote were chock full of God's truth, some quoted straight out of the Holy Scriptures. Occasionally, Dad would even get to preach, and when he did, his favorite passage to preach from was Psalm 1. I remember him talking about the huge trees planted by the river that had to be blasted out of the ground with dynamite, because the root systems were so vast and strong that even the giant earth moving Caterpillar tractors could not drag them up out of the river bank. I cannot think of a better illustration of the strength and fortitude that is provided by a steady, balanced, nutritional diet on the Word of God. Just look at the recipe for this kind of success, it is found in verse 2: *"But his delight is in the law of the LORD; and in His law doth he meditate day and night."*

Let's unpack what verse 3 says about this tree:

1. Planted! Who planted this tree? God, of course!

2. Located by the source of nutrition! God plants where His provision sustains!

3. Abundant! God's Word brings forth fruit. He promises His word will not return to Him void! (Isaiah 55:11, see below)

4. No withering! Don't you want to be an evergreen for Jesus?

5. Thriving! What if everything you did prospered? Are you ready to sign up yet???

Have you heard the story about the two warring dogs inside each one of us? You know, the good dog and the bad dog? They fight for control in our lives. Which dog will win? The one you feed the most, that's who! We must make a conscious, consistent, and concentrated choice to feed the good dog a steady diet of what he needs: the ultimate expression of his Master's love, The Word of God. How far do your roots go down?

Isaiah 55:11   So shall My word be that goeth forth out of my mouth: it shall not return unto me void, but it shall accomplish that which i please, and it shall prosper in the thing whereunto I sent it.

Isaiah 40:8   The grass withereth, the flower fadeth, but the Word of our God shall stand for ever.

This episode was written by Forrest Dartt, one of the original members of The Dartts.

This song, and its soundtrack (if you want to use it to perform the song yourself) is available for download (just search "The Dartts How far do your roots go down?") from the following music subscription services: Amazon Music, Apple Music, iTunes, Spotify, and Youtube Music

Now

Looking behind, all you seem to find

Is sorrow and pain, there is no peace of mind.

And looking ahead to a future that seems dead,

You feel you're living your life with nothing to gain

but something needs to be said for...

Now, now is the time to look to,

We have urgent business to attend to.

Look to Jesus and He will lift you and carry you

and help you through.

Now is the time to look to.

Looking at the past, a darkened shadow has been cast.

Let His light shine through again, to find a peace that will last,

And looking on before, you aren't sure of what's in store,

Don't be afraid to fight your battle

when Christ has already won the war, for...

Tracy Dartt and Forrest Dartt

Now, now is the time to look to,

We have urgent business to attend to.

Look to Jesus and He will lift you and carry you

and help you through.

Now is the time to look to.

You can begin again and start anew,

Just turn it over to the one who died for you.

The past is gone, the future is not yet,

God has a plan for your life that's already set, for...

Now, now is the time to look to,

we have urgent business to attend to.

Look to Jesus and He will lift you and carry you

and help you through.

Now is the time to look to.

Words and music by Forrest Dartt   Copyright 1995

Now   Forrest Dartt:

*Psalm 39:7   And **now**, Lord, what wait I for? my hope is in thee.*

When I was in high school, I remember listening to a friend who told me they had already made so many mistakes that God couldn't possibly have any good use for them. I was heartbroken to think someone so young could feel like that: used up chances in a mistake filled past, and unusable beyond hope with an unattainable future. This is one of the Devil's best 'magic' tricks, to get you to miss what God has for you right now, distracting you to be consumed by past failures you are powerless to undo, or anxieties and fears about things that may never even happen at all.

Putting your faith and trust in God means shifting your focus away from yourself and onto Him. When I am focused on my own past, it is difficult to see past my own failures, but when I focus on God's past, it is impossible to miss the fact that He never abandons or fails his children. *Psalm 37:25* says, *"I have been young, and now am old; yet have I not seen the righteous forsaken, nor his seed begging bread."* When I focus on my own limited ability to anticipate and successfully navigate upcoming obstacles, it is easy to become anxious and pessimistic about the future possibilities; however, when I fix my gaze upon the Lord's promises, I see His plans for me are better than the future I could have imagined for myself. *John 10:10* states: *"The thief cometh not, but for to steal, and to kill, and to destroy: I am come that they might have life, and that they might have it more abundantly."*

Let me ask you something: what have you lost that God cannot restore? Consider the book of Job, and you will find a man who lost his family, his fortune, the respect of his friends, and his good health. But God was faithful to Job, who would not be swayed to speak foolishness against his Lord, and God rewarded Job by giving him twice what he had lost (read *Job 42:10-17* if you don't have time to read the whole thing). God has proven Himself faithful in the past, and He has promised you future victories against the world *(1 John 4:4)*, the devil *(James 4:7)*, and even sin and death *(Romans 8:2)*! You can trust God to take care of your past and your future, so respond to His calling right now.

Will you pray the following prayer with me?

"Oh God, I come to You broken and hopeless, please forgive me and make me whole and fill me with your Spirit. I do not wish to waste another moment focused on myself and my own abilities. Now I want to move forward on Your terms, with a life based on Your words, Your provision, Your will, Your blessings, and Your promises. Help me to be faithful and make me a blessing to others, and I will trust you to complete the good work that you started in me. In Jesus name I pray, amen!"

Philippians 1:6   Being confident of this very thing, that He which hath begun a good work in you will perform it until the day of Jesus Christ:

This episode was written by Forrest Dartt.

This song, and its soundtrack (if you want to use it to perform the song yourself) is available for download (Just search "The Dartts Now") from the following music subscription services: Amazon Music, Apple Music, Itunes, Spotify, and Youtube Music

Let's Form A Committee

At our local church meetin' the preacher gave us a greetin',

He said, Men, let's get down to brass tacks.

We have problems galore, we can't stand any more,

I'm presenting you now with the facts.

Our attendance is down, and the offerings are low,

The roof leaks and our buses won't run.

Every week we go under a thousand or so,

And I just don't know what's to be done. (Umm-ummm!!)

Then said Brother Jones, in impeccable tones,

And a smirk just as big as could be,

I knew all along it would happen like this,

You all should have listened to me. (I told ya!!)

So with great understandin' of these problems demandin',

And the church's best interests in view, (Come on, that's right, brother!)

I move that we promptly establish a group

Who could tell us just what we should do.

Let's form a committee to study the problems,

(Too many problems around here!)

Make a list of suggestions (You're one of 'em!)

Of how we might solve 'em. (Right!)

With the good Lord to guide us, (He'll do it! Amen!)

And an expert or two, (That'll work!)

Let's form a committee, (I think so!)

That's what we should do. (Park there a while!)

(Woo doggies!)(Johnny, stop drawin' in the hymn book!)

(Somebody pray around here!)

Well, a week or so later we gathered together

To see what the committee had found. (Umm-ummm!!)

Then stood Brother West, with his thumb in his vest,

He smiled as he looked all around.

He said, Men, never fear, our solution is clear, (That's right, brother!!)

Our investigation has shown,

We have definite problems, but there's one way to solve them,

(He always says that!)

And only one way alone.

Let's form a committee (Amen!) to study the problems,

(We've never done it that way!)

Make a list of suggestions (I've got my list! Yeah!)

Of how we might solve 'em. (Park there a while!)

With the good Lord to guide us, (Park there for a while! Haaaalelujah!!)

And an expert or two, (I volunteer for that group!)

Let's form a committee, (How 'bout it?)

That's what we should we do. (Yep, think so!!)

(That's good singin' there, folks, good singin'!)

(Hold on there, brother!)

Then said Brother Smith, in a bit of a tiff,

I'm sick, just as sick as can be.

We've got committees for this and committees for that,

And they've done not one thing I can see. ('At's right, brother!)

Well, I've got an opinion and like it or not,

Here's my two cents in the hat. (Put it in my hat, brother!)

Our one biggest problem is too many committees,

Now, what do you all think of that.

Amen! said Brother Sweet, as he stood to his feet.

Brother Smith's hit the nail on the head. (Yeah, yeah, yeah, I did!)

With so many committees in each other's hair,

It's no wonder our church has gone dead. (You're right!)

We must take first things first, and this problem's the worst,

And I think you'll all agree with me, too.(Yeah, I think so!)

We must settle this thing with affirmative action,

Which means there's just one thing to do.

The Words and the Music and the Tears that Fell

Let's form a committee to study the problems,

Make a list of suggestions (Yeah, I did!)

(Anybody got a pen around here?)

Of how we might solve 'em.

With the good Lord to guide us, and an expert or two, (Yep!)

Let's form a committee, (Hallelujah!!) that's what we should do.

(Let's get some pizza around here!)

Let's form a committee to study the problems.

(Too many problems around here!)

Make a list of suggestions (Don't put anchovies on it!)

On how we might solve 'em. (Get your own!!)

With the good Lord to guide us, (Amen! Hallelujah!!)

And an expert or two, (Glo-ry!!)

Let's form a committee (Form it right now, here we go!!)

That's what we should do.

Let's form a committee (I think so! Do you have a problem with that?)

That's what we should do. (I think so! A-ha, yeah, I did!)

(Can we go now? Is the tape still rolling?)

Words and Music by Tracy G. Dartt   Copyright 2000

Let's Form A Committee

A preacher friend of mine accepted the call to pastor a small Baptist church in Louisiana. It was a beautiful little country church, located in a very affluent area. The church was well situated and well founded, but it had a few problems, not the least of which were committees. The church membership was about 50 people, but they had approximately 40 committees. A committee can be of tremendous use to keep things organized, but sometimes a committee can be more of a problem than a help. In this particular church, there had to be a committee meeting to authorize the pastor to buy toilet paper. The pastor managed to convince the church to eliminate most of the committees, and the church began to grow. In less than a year, they built a new sanctuary debt free, and soon grew to an attendance of over 100.

One sunny afternoon, a big Cadillac pulled up outside the pastor's office. Five well-dressed ladies stepped out of the car and came up and knocked on the door. The pastor invited them in and they sat down in his office. Come to find out, they were a self-appointed membership committee, and had gathered a consensus among the older, established members of the church who wanted to stop accepting new members before things got out of control. They wanted to close the membership, as if it were a country club. Apparently, they had lost sight of the church's mission to be an outreach to the world around them. Needless to say, the pastor wasn't around much longer. He was upsetting their lifestyle by bringing in too many sinners.

Matthew 28:18-20   And Jesus came and spoke unto them, saying, All power is given unto me in Heaven and in earth. Go ye therefore, and teach all nations, baptizing them in the name of the Father, and of the Son, and of the Holy Ghost: Teaching them to observe all things whatsoever I have commanded you: and, lo, I am with you alway, even unto the end of the world. Amen.

Matthew 9:10-13   And it came to pass, as Jesus sat at meat in the house, behold, many publicans and sinners came and sat down with him and his disciples. And when the Pharisees saw it, they said unto his disciples, Why eateth your Master with publicans and sinners? But when Jesus heard that, he said unto them, They that be whole need not a physician, but they that are sick. But go ye and learn what that meaneth, I will have mercy, and not sacrifice: for I am not come to call the righteous, but sinners to repentance.

This song, and its soundtrack (if you want to use it to perform the song yourself) is available for download (just search "The Dartts Let's form a committee") from the following music subscription services: Amazon Music, Apple Music, iTunes, Spotify, and Youtube Music

Tracy Dartt and Forrest Dartt

Every Day Is Christmas

Christmas comes just once a year, one solitary day.

It comes and goes so quickly, then it feels so far away.

Most every child has had a wish, a dream that's so sublime.

Wouldn't it be lovely to have Christmas all the time?

Oh, every day is Christmas when you know just how to start

To celebrate the joy of having Jesus in your heart.

And to have the peace of knowing that the Father up above

Looks down upon you every day and covers you with love.

Yes, every good and perfect gift the Father sends your way,

So that you may share this blessed truth with others and say

Knowing Jesus makes each and every day a Merry Christmas day.

Some have never held the truth of Christmas in their grasp.

To trust in God's redeeming gift seems just too great a task.

If they'd only seek the truth, they would surely find

That God has given us the way to have Christmas all the time.

The Words and the Music and the Tears that Fell

Oh, every day is Christmas when you know just how to start

To celebrate the joy of having Jesus in your heart.

And to have the peace of knowing that the Father up above

Looks down upon you every day and covers you with love.

Yes, every good and perfect gift the Father sends your way,

So that you may share this blessed truth with others and say

Knowing Jesus makes each and every day a Merry Christmas day.

Yes, every day is Christmas when you come to understand

That the Father wants to keep you in the hollow of His hand.

Yes, every good and perfect gift the Father sends your way,

So that you may share this blessed truth with others and say.

Knowing Jesus makes each and every day a Merry Christmas Day.

Knowing Jesus makes each and every day a Merry Christmas Day.

Words and Music by Tracy Dartt & Stone Dartt   Copyright 2000

Every Day Is Christmas

Historians have tried for centuries to determine the exact day Christ was born. Most of us celebrate Jesus's birthday on December the 25th, but what if we celebrated Christmas every day? Most of us couldn't afford to buy that many presents! What if we focused less on material gifts, and spent more of our efforts sharing a kind, compassionate, cheerful, and generous spirit in our daily interaction with our fellow man? After all, it is the giving and sharing spirit that matters more than the presents, right? The word Christmas is made from a combination of two words. Christ, our Lord and Savior, and Mass, the celebration of the Eucharist or communion. This ceremony acknowledges the privilege and blessing of becoming one with Christ.

Some time ago, my wife, Sharon, was in a beauty parlor in Sherman, Texas. There was a Christmas parade passing by while she was in the hairdryer. The high school marching band was playing "Joy To The World." A woman sitting close by asked, "Why do they have to play those religious songs every Christmas?" Sad to say, this is an attitude shared by more people than we would expect.

As Christians, we need to celebrate Christ on Christ-mas. There is nothing wrong about giving gifts, after all, God started it all with that first Christmas gift - His own Son, along with the choice to receive the gift of eternal life. We need to remember the gift of God's Son, Jesus, and share his truth and love with others every day of the year! With that in mind, I say to you, "Merry Christmas" - whatever day this happens to be!

James 1:17   Every good gift and every perfect gift is from above, and cometh from the Father of lights, with whom is no variableness neither shadow of turning.

Ephesians 4:7   But unto every one of us is given grace according to the measure of the gift of Christ.

This song is available for download (just search "The Dartts Every day is Christmas") from the following music subscription services: Amazon Music, Apple Music, iTunes, Spotify, and Youtube Music

Mama

I watch the flickering candle as I sit by Mama's bedside

And I hold the gentle hand that's led me through so many years.

And I hear her softly whisper words that break into my heart,

And I vainly try holding back the tears.

She said, Hon, I've always known you'd find Jesus as your own.

And so many times I've prayed that I would live to see the day.

I pray soon we'll meet together on the far side of the river.

Then she gently squeezed my hand, and I wept as Mama cried.

Now the candle is growing dimmer

and Mama's gentle hand grows cold,

And it's hard to face the fact that one so sweet and dear is gone.

And those words she softly whispered

echo deep within my soul.

As I pray, Dear God, forgive me, Jesus, take me as your own.

The Words and the Music and the Tears that Fell

Jesus, Mama never knew that I gave my life to you,

As I sat there by her side on the night that Mama died.

So please tell her we'll meet together on the far side of the river,

'Cause I gave my heart to Jesus on the night that Mama died.

Yes, I gave my heart to Jesus on the night that Mama died.

Words and Music by Tracy G. Dartt   Copyright 1975

Mama

In 1975 my wife, Sharon, and I recorded an album with June Wade and The Country Congregation. We made the recording at Capitol Studio in Hollywood, California. We had a fine crew of professional musicians and a great engineer. It turned out to be an album to be proud of. I had written all but one of the songs on the album. One of my songs was the first recording of God On The Mountain. Another one of the songs was this one, "Mama." I tell the story (in the first person) of a godly mother who is just about to go home to Heaven, as I sit beside her. Mama expresses her longing and prayers for my salvation. As Mama breaths her final breath, I weep and cry out to the Lord to save me, asking Jesus to tell Mama of my decision.

I find no place in the scripture that states that we can communicate with those who have gone on to Heaven before us. We can, however, pray to our Heavenly Father, asking Him to speak to them for us. We have nothing to lose - it's up to the Lord whether or not to fulfill our request.

Many people thought that either I or June Wade had written this song as a personal testimony. This was not the case. However, in my years of ministry I have prayed with many individuals who have asked for prayer for an unsaved loved one, and we've seen many answers to prayer.

I did not grow up in a Christian home. My Mother was saved at the age of nine at a Salvation Army Church in Redwing, Minnesota. Though she was unable to attend regularly, she prayed for me continually, and taught me to believe in God. She taught me to pray a simple prayer every night at bedtime, "Now I lay me down to sleep, I pray the Lord my soul to keep. If I should die before I wake, I pray the Lord my soul to take. God bless Mama, God bless Daddy, and God bless Brother." This helped me to know that God is real, and at the age of 19, I accepted Christ as my own personal Savior.

I had the privilege of baptizing my Mother while I was pastoring a church in central California. She passed away at the age of 96, having lived a full and productive life. Her prayers for me and for our ministry continued all the years of her life.

1 Peter 3:12a   For the eyes of the Lord are over the righteous, and His ears are open unto their prayers.

John 17:20   Neither pray I for these alone, but for them also which shall believe on me through their word.

This song is available to stream (just search "Mama by June wade") on Youtube.com

Daddy Please Love Me

I'm livin' in the same house, just down the hall from you,

I hear everything that you say, watch everything you do.

Sometimes when you're not lookin' I walk around in your shoes.

You see I've got your eyes and I've got your smile,

And I wanna be just like you.

But, Daddy, please love me. Daddy please love me,

Daddy please hold me, and tell me that you're proud of me.

'Cause I gotta go out into, this cold hard world,

I'll be livin' my life in this hurtin' world,

And I wanna go out into, this big bad world with your love.

I won't be here forever. It won't be long,

'Til I'm all grown up, and I'll be movin' on.

Have you got somethin' to tell me?

'Cause I've got something I need to hear.

Tracy Dartt and Forrest Dartt

Please tell me that you love me, Daddy,

Tell me while you hold me near.

But, Daddy, please love me. Daddy please love me,

Daddy please hold me, and tell me that you're proud of me.

'Cause I gotta go out into, this cold hard world,

I'll be livin' my life in this hurtin' world,

And I wanna go out into, this big bad world with your love.

The things you say about me,

whether or not you mean it,

whether or not it's true,

Those words that you say,

go down deep inside me,

and you know that's what I think of me too.

So, Daddy, please love me. Daddy please love me,

Daddy please hold me, and tell me that you're proud of me.

The Words and the Music and the Tears that Fell

'Cause I gotta go out into, this cold hard world,

I'll be livin' my life in this hurtin' world,

And I wanna go out into, this big bad world with your love.

Words and music by Don Dartt   Copyright 2002

Daddy Please Love Me   Don Dartt:

   Growing up on the road during the years of my father's solo ministry, my siblings, Peachy, Frosty, Stoney and I, had the opportunity to meet many many new friends around the country, most of them the children of Pastors and Church Leaders. Often we were invited to their homes for meals and sometimes even got to spend the night. We had tons of fun, but these visits also gave us a fly-on-the-wall glimpse into the private lives and relationship dynamics of many different families.

   I'd love to tell you that all of those families exhibited loving, respectful, and nurturing environments that were a "cut above" what the rest of us experience. That would be false. The truth is that behind the scenes, those families were very much like the everyday variety of families you may have encountered in your life. They ranged from amazing, to good, to marginally okay, to just plain awful, and the responsibility for that has to fall on the parents.

   I'm not trying to beat up on the parents of "PKs". They live in glass houses, there's a lot of pressure, there's a lot of "living-up-to-expectations" and "people-pleasing" going on. My point is, even for people who have dedicated their lives to the ministry, the ministry to their own children still requires an extra measure of dedication and intentionality... just like the rest of us.

I have heard parents say some really awful things to their kids. I'm no better, just ask my two adult kids. Taylor and Rachel grew up on the road as well, during the years that I "walked around in my Daddy's shoes" and did my own solo ministry. It was during this time that I wrote this song, to remind myself that the words I say to them as a parent go down deep inside their hearts and minds, and become part of how they see themselves.

Words are powerful, and hurtful words can have a major impact on the life of the receiver. The scary thing is, even those words flung out in a moment, in anger and in haste - or even just as a joke - can burn into the minds and weigh heavily on our children throughout their lives. How much better would it be to burn in words of encouragement and support, positive words that build confidence and trust in the relationship. How much better would it be to hold them close and say, "I love you", I'm so proud of you".

I thank God for my Daddy. I'm thankful he's still with us. I'm thankful for the great relationship we've enjoyed over the years. It hasn't always been perfect - we're human you know - but I'm now in my 50s and he tells me he loves me and is proud of me every time I see him, every time we text, talk by phone, and every time he leaves me a voice message. I don't have to ask. I know my Daddy loves me.

This episode was written by Don Dartt, eldest son of Tracy and Sharon Dartt

This song is available for download (just search "Don Dartt Daddy Please Love Me") from the following music subscription services: Amazon Music, Apple Music, iTunes, Spotify, and Youtube Music.

In The Eye Of The Storm

Can you remember the day

nothing seemed to go your way?

you thought all hope was lost and gone

you had no words, you had no song

Do you remember the place

you said I'll quit I'll end the race?

I can't go on today,

another time I'll find some way

That's when your heart began to cry,

so you looked toward the sky

your soul began to weep,

Then you heard your God speak...

In the eye of the storm,

when you're confused and torn

Just look to me, I'll help you see.

I'll give you what you need

Tracy Dartt and Forrest Dartt

In the eye of the storm,

I'll see you through,

I've been there too,

I'll take care of you...

(He is there) When I need Him

(He is there) When I call

(There is no need to fear) He is my All and All

In the eye of the storm,

when you're confused and torn

Just look to me, I'll help you see.

I'll give you what you need

In the eye of the storm, I'll see you through,

I've been there too, I'll take care of you...

I'll see you through, I'll take care of you...

Words and Music by BJ Speer   Copyright 2013

70

In The Eye Of The Storm   BJ Speer:

I joined the Dartts music group in December of 2004, but I also officially became part of their family. They have adopted me, taken me under their wings, and loved me as their own, and I am forever grateful. We have been through many 3-6 month long tours, lived with each other on a 45ft tour bus which permanently qualifies you as family!

In the Eye of the Storm was the very first song I ever wrote. I was going through a dark place in my life after finishing high school, and not knowing what I wanted to do with my life. I had no idea what God wanted from me or for me. I was lost, I was searching, and I was lonely. I was going through a hurricane of feelings, and somehow found myself in the middle of the storm with what seemed like no way out.

I remember going into my room, crying with my hands up in the air, begging for God to deliver me from this place. I ended up writing these words down on paper in about 10 minutes. At this time in my life, I had grown up on the road into a musical family, but I never sang myself. I was scared of being in front of people, scared of what people thought and scared of sharing a gift that God had given me. I ended up taking a year off before going to college, taking care of my mother who was ill at the time. During that time I found my way through the storm, and God was my lighthouse.

During my first year of Bible College, I showed this song to a friend, who listened to my melody, and played it ever so beautifully in the educational auditorium. My words had jumped off the pages, and into a song. I had the wonderful opportunity to record it with my family on a project my Dad was working on called, "Keep Believing". The message is still relevant today... That in the Eye of the Storm, God is there, guiding, directing, leading and loving us to safer shores once again.

Luke 8:23-24   But as they sailed he fell asleep: and there came down a storm of wind on the lake; and they were filled with water, and were in jeopardy. And they came to him, and awoke him, saying, Master, master, we perish. Then he arose, and rebuked the wind and the raging of the water: and they ceased, and there was a calm.

This episode was written by BJ Speer of the Dartts.

This song is available for download (just search "BJ Speer In the eye of the storm") from the following music subscription services: Amazon Music, Apple Music, iTunes, Spotify, and Youtube Music

He'll Take Us To A Better Place

We're not here forever

upon this Earth below

Someday we'll be leaving,

and I know where I'll go

I am bound for Heaven,

Jesus told me so

I have been forgiven,

that is why I know

He'll take us to a better place,

we'll look upon His loving face

He said that we could leave this world below

when we complete this Earthy race

We'll stand before Him one by one,

there'll be rewards for what we've done

Wouldn't you like to go and be with Him you know,

He said He'd take us to a better place

There is no perfection

in this world below

the longer that your living,

the more you're sure to know

better days are coming

for those who love the Lord

Jesus made a promise,

we can rest assured

He'll take us to a better place,

we'll look upon His loving face

He said that we could leave this world below

when we complete this Earthy race

We'll stand before Him one by one,

there'll be rewards for what we've done

Wouldn't you like to go and be with Him you know,

He said He'd take us to a better place

Words and Music by Sharon Dartt   Copyright 2016

He'll Take Us To A Better Place

II Peter 3:13   Nevertheless we, according to his promise, look for new heavens and a new earth, wherein dwelleth righteousness.

It's tough to build a better place. You can have backed up sewage, traffic jams, pot holes, insect and rodent infestation, not to mention earthquakes, wildfires, and extreme weather events. Later you will deal with urban sprawl, large corporations moving out and leaving an undesirable void that may invite inner city poverty, crime, and political corruption. You'd think over time we would learn our lessons, make better plans and choices, and finally produce Utopia, but not since the Garden of Eden have we ever been with a longshot of paradise.

Those of us who have loved ones who have gone on before take great comfort in knowing that our loved ones are already in the presence of God, which we really cannot even imagine! Jesus promised His disciples that He would go and prepare a place for us. He has been working on that place for two thousand of our years. Now, if God created this world for us in only six days, how much grander will Heaven be in comparison? He has invited everyone to come and join Him, and there will be plenty of room for all who will believe in Christ and accept His free gift of salvation.

The older we get, the more delightful it is to anticipate the relocation into God's eternal presence. We have many friends and family members to greet us when we arrive, but we must never cease to reach out to those around us who are not yet prepared for that journey. We must be forgiven of our sins to be admitted to the Kingdom that our Holy God who has prepared us. We can never lose sight of our purpose in this world as Ambassadors for Jesus Christ, and we must bear humble witness of the mercy and grace that God has so freely offered to us all. Please remember to represent your new neighborhood to your fellow man, and let them know they are welcome to join us in Heaven as well!

John 3:3   Jesus answered and said unto him, Verily, verily, I say unto thee, Except a man be born again, he cannot see the kingdom of God.

I Corinthians 2:7-9   But we speak the wisdom of God in a mystery, even the hidden wisdom, which God ordained before the world unto our glory: Which none of the princes of this world knew: for had they known it, they would not have crucified the Lord of glory. But as it is written, Eye hath not seen, nor ear heard, neither have entered into the heart of man, the things which God hath prepared for them that love him.

This song is available for download (just search "The Dartts He'll Take us to a better place") from the following music subscription services: Amazon Music, Apple Music, iTunes, Spotify, and Youtube Music

Shoutin' Ground

Sometimes I get nervous when I sit in the service

Of some Baptist churches I know.

My cup starts to fill and I can't still,

I can't keep from lettin' it show.

The ushers are frownin', they think that I'm clownin'

I try not to make a sound.

But there's no use concealin' the joy I'm feelin'

When I'm standin' on shoutin' ground.

I'm standin' on shoutin' ground,

That's the spot where the blessin's come down.

When the blessin's free pour down on me

I'm standin' on shoutin' ground.

I'm standin' on shoutin' ground,

Runnin' over with joy that I've found.

It's easy to see God's blessin' me

And I'm standin' on shoutin' ground.

Tracy Dartt and Forrest Dartt

If you find it distressing when God starts in blessing

To be strictly confined to your pew,

You don't have to be quiet, but don't start a riot,

There are a few things you can do.

If you find it's no use, go ahead, cut loose

With a hearty amen or two.

But if that doesn't do ya, shout hallelujah

'Cuz you're standin' on shoutin' ground.

I'm standin' on shoutin' ground,

That's the spot where the blessin's come down.

When the blessin's free pour down on me

I'm standin' on shoutin' ground.

I'm standin' on shoutin' ground,

Runnin' over with joy that I've found.

It's easy to see God's blessin' me

And I'm standin' on shoutin' ground.

Words and Music by Tracy G. Dartt   Copyright 2004

Shoutin' Ground

This little song is a tongue-in-cheek comment on those Baptist churches who are afraid of any emotion or demonstration of excitement in the church service. I'm free to write this, because I am a Baptist myself. I consider myself to be a "Bapticostal." If a person doesn't have enough of the Holy Spirit, (or should I say the Holy Spirit doesn't have enough of the person) to generate a little excitement over the moving of the Holy Spirit, I wonder if they are really born again.

1 Samuel 4:4-7   So the people sent to Shiloh, that they might bring from thence the ark of the Lord of hosts, which dwelt between the cherubims: and the two sons of Eli, Hophni and Phinehas, were there with the ark of the covenant of God. And when the ark of the covenant of the Lord came into the camp, all Israel shouted with a great shout, so that the earth rang again. And when the Philistines heard the noise of the shout, they said, What meaneth the noise of this great shout in the camp of the Hebrews? And they understood that the ark of the Lord had come into the camp. And the Philistines were afraid, for they said, God is come into the camp. And they said, Woe unto us! for there hath not been such a thing heretofore.

In this scripture, 1 Samuel 4:4-7, the children of Israel became so excited when the ark of the covenant came into the camp, they all shouted. The noise of their shouting was so loud in Ebenezer that the Philistines heard them two miles away in Aphek and became afraid. We as Christians should never be afraid to get excited about the Lord, but the emotion needs to come sincerely from the heart and from the Holy Spirit.

In this incident recorded in 1 Samuel, the shouting was loud, but the hearts of the people were not right. This was proven because God allowed them to be defeated by the Philistines. King David, on the other hand, in 2 Samuel chapter 6, brought the ark into the City of David, next to Jerusalem. The scripture says that all the house of Israel came with him; there was shouting, trumpets, joy, sacrifices along the way, and even dancing. The procession was so joyful, that it even inspired me to write the song "David's Polka!!" The joy of the Lord was evident in Israel, and the blessings of the Lord were upon King David and his people.

2 Samuel 6:12b-15   So David went and brought up the ark of God from the house of Obed-Edom into the city of David with gladness. And it was so, that when they that bare the ark of the Lord had gone six paces, he sacrificed oxen and fatlings and David danced before the Lord with all his might; and David was girded with a linen ephod. So David and all the house of Israel brought up the ark of the Lord with shouting, and with the sound of the trumpet.

Years ago, as we were traveling full time on the road with our children, we were in a revival meeting where the song service was very spirited and joyful. As we were singing, "I'm living on the mountain, underneath a cloudless sky," the whole church shouted "Praise God!" at the end of the line. Just a couple of weeks later, we were in another church, and the congregation was singing that same song. When we got to the end of the line, "underneath a cloudless sky," our 8 year old son, Frosty, yelled "Praise God" at the top of his lungs. But he was the only one out of the crowd of several hundred people to do so, and he was so embarrassed that he began to cry. Folks around us began to laugh, and the preacher stopped the song. "Don't cry, little fella," he said to Frosty. "We all should be saying that." Then he had the song leader repeat the chorus, and had everyone say "Praise God!" together where Frosty had yelled it out.

This song, is available for download (just search "The Dartts Shoutin' ground") from the following music subscription services: Amazon Music, Apple Music, iTunes, Spotify, and Youtube Music

The Flag and the Cross

What does it mean to a man

to see a flag waving high?

He thinks of his blessed homeland

and the men who had to die

To preserve him the right

to believe what he wants to

And say what he wants to say.

That's what the flag means to me today.

What does it mean to a man

to see an old rugged cross?

He thinks of the God who gave His Son

to die for the souls of the lost,

That they'd have the right

to love Him and serve Him

And from sin be set free.

That's what the cross means to someone like me.

Tracy Dartt and Forrest Dartt

Thank God for the flag that gives me the right

To worship the Man on the cross.

Long may it wave o'er the Land of the Brave,

We pray that these rights won't be lost.

Thank God for the cross that bore our Savior that day at Calvary.

Thank God for the flag and the cross.

Thank God for the flag and the cross.

Thank God for the flag and the cross for they gave me liberty.

Words and Music by Tracy G. Dartt   Copyright 2000

The Flag and the Cross

1 Corinthians 1:18   For the preaching of the cross is to them that perish foolishness; but unto us which are saved it is the power of God.

The cross, to the Christian, is a symbol of power, but not power as the world sees it. It is the symbol of the power of the Gospel (good news.) The good news is that the acceptance of the sacrifice that Christ made on the cross has the power to free us from the bondage and the penalty of sin. We are changed from death unto life by the indwelling power of the Holy Spirit, making us a new creature, a new creation - and giving us a new life and purpose for living.

2 Corinthians 5:17   Therefore if any man be in Christ, he is a new creature: old things are passed away; behold, all things are become new.

Some would say that the cross is a symbol of execution and death. Crucifixion was the method of execution used by the Roman Empire, but the method used by the Jews was stoning. Jesus was tried before the High Priest and The Council of the Jews, and then sent to be tried by Pontius Pilate, the Roman Governor. After questioning Jesus Pilate declared, "I find no fault in this man." He then took water and washed his hands before the multitude, saying, "I am innocent of the blood of this just person: see ye to it." (Matthew 27:24b) Jesus was condemned to death, not because of His guilt, but because of the cry of the crowd, "Let Him be crucified." Jesus was condemned by the world power but betrayed by His own people. The question is, who was responsible for His death? Because His life was given as a sacrifice to pay for our sin, the blame might be ours. But Jesus said this:

John 10:17-18   Therefore doth my Father love me, because I lay down my life, that I might take it again. No man taketh it from me, but I lay it down of myself. I have power to lay it down, and I have power to take it again. This commandment have I received of my Father.

Our nation's flag is the symbol of a nation of free people. The stripes represent the original thirteen colonies, and the fifty states of the union are represented by the fifty stars. Our Constitution and our Bill of Rights guarantee us rights like the freedom of assembly, freedom of speech, and the right to worship as we please. It is up to us to make use of our right to vote. It is also our responsibility to pray for those in authority over us, lest our freedoms be taken away. To a greater extent than we realize, the freedoms and success of our free country are dependent upon our faithful obedience to God's commands to us as Christians.

Proverbs 29:2   When the righteous are in authority, the people rejoice: but when the wicked beareth rule, the people mourn.

1 Peter 5:8   Be sober, be vigilant; because your adversary the devil, as a roaring lion, walketh about, seeking whom he may devour:

1 Timothy 2:1-3   I exhort therefore, that, first of all, supplications, prayers, intercessions, and giving of thanks, be made for all men; for kings, and for all that are in authority; that we may lead a quiet and peaceable life in all godliness and honesty. For this is good and acceptable in the sight of God our Savior;

Proverbs 14:34   Righteousness exalteth a nation: but sin is a reproach to any people.

2 Chronicles 7:14   If my people, which are called by my name, shall humble themselves, and pray, and seek my face, and turn from their wicked ways; then will I hear from Heaven, and will forgive their sin, and will heal their land.

This song is available for download (just search "The Dartts the flag and the cross") from the following music subscription services: Amazon Music, Apple Music, iTunes, Spotify, and Youtube Music

Bring Back The Children

Son, It's time to bring back the children.

Seems like yesterday You came back home.

But years have passed and now they're all ready

And it's time, My Son, to gather Your own.

Father, I'm ready, and I'm on my way

How long I have waited to hear You say

The very last name was recorded today

And it's time, yes, it's time to bring back the children.

Children, I'm coming, the hour is here.

In less than a heartbeat I'll be holding you near.

There'll be no more sorrow, and there'll be no more tears

For it's time, yes, it's time to bring back the children.

Son, it's time to bring back the children.

Seems like yesterday You came back home.

Tracy Dartt and Forrest Dartt

But years have passed and now they're all ready

And it's time, My Son,

Yes, it's time, My Son, to gather Your own.

Words and Music by Sharon M. Dartt   Copyright 1976

Bring Back The Children

1 Thessalonians 4:16-18   For the Lord himself shall descend from heaven with a shout, with the voice of the archangel, and with the trump of God: and the dead in Christ shall rise first: Then we which are alive and remain shall be caught up together with them in the clouds, to meet the Lord in the air: and so shall we ever be with the Lord. Wherefore comfort one another with these words.

I remember when we were living in Maysville, Oklahoma fifty years ago. Our son, Don, was in Kindergarten. When we would come to pick him up after school, he would be so happy and excited to be picked up. He would come running to greet us, and he couldn't wait to get home so he could show us his work paper or his project that he had completed. He would grin from ear to ear when we told him it was good and how proud we were of him.

Someday soon I believe it will be time for the Lord to come and gather His children: all those who are born again. I am looking forward to that day, and I am praying that I will hear God say, *"Well done, thou good and faithful servant: thou hast been faithful over a few things I will make thee ruler over many things: enter thou into the joy of thy lord."* (Matthew 25:21)

The Words and the Music and the Tears that Fell

When my wife, Sharon, wrote this song, I was traveling with my family as a soloist. I recorded it on one of my first solo albums. It was well received so we decided to record it again with our Dartt Family Quartet on our Shed A Little Light album. Twenty more years have come and gone since then. We included this song in our concerts all the way up to our retirement in 2018, and still we are waiting for that trumpet sound. Oh, how we'd love to hear that sound today! Unfortunately, many of us still have friends and loved ones that have not yet believed the truth of the Gospel. We do know that there will come a time when the Father will say to the Son, "Go and gather the children!" Let's earnestly pray and ask God for an opportunity to share the good news of God's saving grace before it is too late.

John 1:12   But as many as received Him, to them gave He power to become the sons of God, even to them that believe on his name.

Matthew 25:13   Watch therefore, for ye know neither the day nor the hour wherein the Son of man cometh.

This song, and its soundtrack (if you want to use it to perform the song yourself) is available for download (just search "The Dartts Bring back the children") from the following music subscription services: Amazon Music, Apple Music, iTunes, Spotify, and Youtube Music

Tracy Dartt and Forrest Dartt

Running Home

For Stoney Dartt and BJ Speer

I want this to be my final day of darkness

Could this be the conclusion of my pain?

Hope this is the last time that I see you through my tears

There's nothing good left in me to remain

I want this to be the last place that I suffer

I want yours to be the last hand that I hold

This will be the last time that you're cleaning up my mess

I'm praying for my ending to unfold

We said every prayer we could think of

Never did you leave me all alone

Letting go of you will be the hardest thing I've done

But I'm not giving up, I'm running home

The Words and the Music and the Tears that Fell

Please let this be the last pill that I swallow

I want this to be the final smile I fake

Let me feel your arms around me just this one last time

Now I pray the Lord my soul to take

This will be the last wish that I utter

I want yours to be the last face that I saw

Close my eyes forever and my life goes flashing by

This will be the final breath I draw

We said every prayer we could think of

Never did you leave me all alone

Letting go of you will be the hardest thing I've done

But I'm not giving up, I'm running home

No, I'm not giving up, I'm running home

Promise I'll be waiting when you get here

He let me save your place nearby the throne

I'll be cheering for you as you press on toward the goal

But I can't wait to see you running home,

No, I can't wait 'til you'll be running home

Words and Music by Forrest Dartt   Copyright 2021

Running Home   Forrest Dartt:

II Timothy 4:6-8, 18   For I am now ready to be offered, and the time of my departure is at hand. I have fought a good fight, I have finished my course, I have kept the faith: Henceforth there is laid up for me a crown of righteousness, which the Lord, the righteous judge, shall give me at that day: and not to me only, but unto all them also that love his appearing.

My brother, Stoney, was diagnosed with a rare form of cancer a couple of years ago. There were possibilities of experimental treatments enough to give us hope that he might be around for a long while, but nothing seemed to work. Everything the doctors tried to do kept making it worse and accelerating Stoney's demise. My brother passed away on July 6, 2021 at the Cancer Treatment Centers of America in Newnan, Georgia.

BJ Speer, who is also one of the Dartts, was with Stoney every step of the way. He was Stoney's caregiver, and BJ was the quintessential *"friend that sticketh closer than a brother"* that is mentioned in *Proverbs 18:24.* He made sure every avenue of treatment and relief was provided for Stoney, and no one could have done it better.

Of course, none of us wanted for Stoney's end to ever come, but there comes a moment when the tug-of-war between the forces of life and death becomes too much for the physical body to endure. When Stoney got to that point, he knew it was time to unplug all the tubes and wires and place himself solely in God's hands. He rounded the final corner and ran down to the finish wire. He ran really fast. It didn't take long. Stoney breathed his final breath while BJ played the music of the Dartts, a song called "Count on the Shepherd" from the Dartts "Go Ye Into All the World" album.

We will all make our run sooner or later. Some of us may have a chance to choose our last few steps the way that Stoney did, but many of us will suddenly be called away without warning, without a pleasant soundtrack, and without the benefit or comfort of a loved one present. When that time comes for you, I hope you know you are running home to your Savior's loving arms and an eternity in the presence of God. If you are not sure if you are prepared for that moment, then you are not! Take a moment to invite Jesus Christ to be the Lord and Savior of your life. Believe in Him with your heart. Confess with your Mouth that He is Lord. He will seal your redemption with His righteous Holy Spirit, and He will deliver your soul from death, Hell, and the grave. He will deliver you home!

This episode was written by Forrest Dartt.

This song is available to stream (just search "Running Home by Forrest Dartt") on Youtube.com

Safe Harbor

Out adrift on life's dark sea

The raging storm had carried me

Far away from the land of hope and dreams.

I had planned my course alone

But it took me far from home

And the things that my Father planned for me.

But at last I saw the light like a beacon in the night,

Guiding me to safe harbor where my soul could firmly anchor.

God had sent His only Son to light the way for me and everyone

Who is seeking out safe harbor for the soul.

The winds of life have not blown fair.

The storm has brought you to despair.

But don't give up for your Father hears your cry.

And you are nearer than you know

To safe harbor for your soul

The Words and the Music and the Tears that Fell

And the Father is not willing you should die.

And at last I saw the light like a beacon in the night,

Guiding me to safe harbor where my soul could firmly anchor.

God had sent His only Son to light the way for me and everyone

Who is seeking out safe harbor for the soul.

God had sent His only Son to light the way for me and everyone

Who is seeking out safe harbor for the soul.

Words and Music by Tracy G. Dartt   Copyright 1998

Safe Harbor

Every once in a while, my daughter, Peachy, and I will sit for hours watching a show called "The Deadliest Catch." We find it interesting that the crews on those boats risk their lives, fishing for crabs in the dangerous waters of the Behring Sea. If they are fortunate, they can earn enough money in a week or two to last them several months. But it seems that in each season of the show, a ship sinks or someone is killed.

Psalms 107: 23-28   They that go down to the sea in ships, that do business in great waters; These see the works of the Lord, and His wonders in the deep. For He commandeth, and raiseth the stormy wind, which lifteth up the waves thereof. They mount up to the heaven, they go down again to the depths: their soul is melted because of trouble. They reel to and fro, and stagger like a drunken man, and are their wits' end. Then they cry out to the Lord in their trouble, and He bringeth them out of their distresses.

Our singing group, The Dartts, was fortunate to be invited to sing on several ocean cruises. Every night after dinner there would be a gospel concert, featuring several different groups. Each cruise was a wonderful experience. Each ship was amazing. The accommodations and the food were extraordinary. However, on one cruise to the Caribbean, we were in a smaller ship and ran into some rough waters. We were just south of the Grand Cayman Islands, in the deepest part of the Atlantic Ocean. It was difficult to stand up without holding on to something.

In the book of Acts, chapter 27, we see the apostle Paul being taken by ship to Italy, to face a trial before Caesar. Although Paul had warned the ship's owner and the centurion who held him in charge that there was great danger ahead, they would not listen. The ship ran into a great storm, called Euroclydon. All aboard were fearful for their lives, but an angel of the Lord appeared to Paul and told him that all on board would be saved, but the ship would be lost. They had been trying to reach a safe harbor called Phenice, to winter there in spite of Paul's warnings. The angel's words to Paul proved true, and though the ship broke up and sank, not a man was lost, but all came safely to an island called Melita, where a group of natives received them.

You may have found yourself adrift on life's sea. You need to find the one truly safe harbor. Anchor your soul in the Haven of Rest. In Christ there is peace and protection and provision. Don't be a castaway. Find the eye of the storm which lies in the center of God's will for your life.

Acts 27:22-24   And now I exhort you to be of good cheer: for there shall be no loss of any man's life among you, but of the ship. For there stood by me this night the angel of God, whose I am, and whom I serve, saying, fear not, Paul; thou must be brought before Caesar: and, lo, God hath given thee all them that sail with thee.

This song, and its soundtrack (if you want to use it to perform the song yourself) is available for download (just search "the Dartts Safe harbor") from the following music subscription services: Amazon Music, Apple Music, iTunes, Spotify, and Youtube Music

Tracy Dartt and Forrest Dartt

A Matter of Policy (Deacon Song)

I noticed something strange on my way to church last Sunday.

Billows of smoke came pouring from the door.

I ran up to tell our leading deacon,

Something should be done, the church is on fire for sure.

He said, That's a point well put and a timely suggestion

That we'll bring up at the very next meeting

Of the board of deacons, a week from Tuesday,

I don't know why, it's just church policy

At the First Naza-Metha-Bapticostal-

Seventh Day-Orthodox-Luthaterian,

Non-Denominational Church of Our Lady of the Mind.

Well, we were back the very next Sunday

In a tent bought and paid for by the building fund.

I stood up to tell the congregation

There's a tornado coming, everybody run.

The Words and the Music and the Tears that Fell

They said, That's a point well put and a timely suggestion

That we'll bring up at the very next meeting

Of the board of deacons, a week from Tuesday,

I don't know why, it's just church policy

At the First Naza-Metha-Bapticostal-

Seventh Day-Orthodox-Luthaterian,

Non-Denominational Church of Our Lady of the Mind.

We had an open air meeting the very next Sunday,

When a trumpet blew and the clouds were rolled away.

I stood up to tell the congregation

Lift up your heads, the Lord has come today.

They said, That's a point well put and a timely suggestion

That we'll bring up at the very next meeting

Of the board of deacons, a week from Tuesday,

I don't know why, it's just church policy

At the First Naza-Metha-Bapticostal-

Tracy Dartt and Forrest Dartt

Seventh Day-Orthodox-Luthaterian,

Non-Denominational Church of Our Lady of the Mind.

Words and Music by Tracy G. Dartt   Copyright 1977

A Matter of Policy (Deacon Song)

A matter of policy has been one of our most popular songs since the very beginning of our music ministry. I used to think that it might be the one song that I would be remembered for. But that was before God On The Mountain became well known. That was a relief!

Some churches like to laugh at themselves (a little). We sometimes bind ourselves with a set of rules that quench the moving of the Holy Spirit. We focus on methods instead of the Master. A pastor friend of mine took a church in Louisiana some years back. This church had a rule book to cover every possible situation. (Sad to say, it was not the Bible.) There seemed to be a lack of love and compassion, just judgement and making sure that everyone measured up. The board had to meet even to approve the purchase of toilet paper. My friend didn't stay there very long.

At another church, (with a very wealthy membership) a new pastor had been winning many people to Christ and baptizing them. The congregation was growing so quickly that the church auditorium was not big enough to hold the crowd. To accommodate the growth, a beautiful new sanctuary had been built. One afternoon a group of well-dressed ladies pulled into the parking lot of the church in a big Cadillac. They entered the church and knocked on the door of the pastor's study. As he opened the door one of the ladies began,

"We'd like to speak to you about something. The church is growing too fast, and we feel that it's time to close the membership." The pastor couldn't believe what he was hearing. Close the membership?? Just as if it were a country club??

Of course, the real problem was that the increase in membership diluted the voting power of those who held control of the church. Instead of rejoicing at the number of new converts, they had become uneasy about the direction things might take in the future. As Christians we need to focus on the fact that our churches, our gatherings, are all about growth, both spiritually as individuals, and growth in numbers as we reach out to win others to Christ.

Romans 12:1-2   I beseech you therefore, brethren, by the mercies of God, that ye present your bodies a living sacrifice, holy, acceptable unto God, which is your reasonable service. And be not confirmed to this world: but be ye transformed by the renewing of your mind, that ye may prove what is that good, and acceptable, and perfect, will of God.

Proverbs 22:2   The rich and the poor meet together: the Lord is the maker of them all.

Galatians 4:9-11   But now, after that ye have known God, or rather are known of God, how turn ye again to the weak and beggarly elements, whereunto ye desire again to be in bondage? Ye observe days, and months, and times, and years. I am afraid of you, lest I have bestowed upon you labor in vain.

This song, and its soundtrack (if you want to use it to perform the song yourself) is available for download (just search "the Dartts a matter of policy") from the following music subscription services: Amazon Music, Apple Music, iTunes, Spotify, and Youtube Music

Tracy Dartt and Forrest Dartt

Foundations of Faith

Jesus once told the story of so foolish a man,

Who had built him a house on foundations of sand;

When the rains had descended and the flood waters came,

The foolish man's house fell apart to his shame.

I'm building upon the Foundations of Faith,

I believe in the Savior and I've made Him my Lord;

For nothing can shake the Foundations of Faith,

And I'm placing my trust in my God's Holy Word.

There is more to the story for a wise man one day,

Also built him a house on a rock so they say;

When the rains had descended and the flood waters came,

The wise man's new house stood the storm's mighty rage.

I'm building upon the Foundations of Faith,

I believe in the Savior and I've made Him my Lord;

The Words and the Music and the Tears that Fell

For nothing can shake the Foundations of Faith,

And I'm placing my trust in my God's Holy Word.

Words and Music by Tracy G. Dartt   Copyright 1973

Foundations of Faith

We all need to build our lives upon the only sure foundation, faith in Jesus Christ our Savior and the Holy Spirit inspired Word of God. If Jesus is not the Son of God, the Anointed One, The Christ, Immanuel (God with us), and the Bible is not the Word of God speaking to us, then our faith is in vain. But the truth is, He is all of these things, and the Bible is the Word of God.

In the building of anything, the foundation is of primary importance. If the foundation is weak, the entire structure will eventually collapse. Earlier this year that very thing occurred when a large apartment building collapsed in Florida, due to a faulty foundation.

When I was in high school and on summer vacation, my cousin, Bruce, offered me a job. He was building an addition on a cabin in the mountains of southern California. He said, "Did you ever operate a Mexican drag line?" Of course, I had never heard of that. I pictured myself operating some big digging machine. So, off we went, high up into the mountains away from everything. I soon found out that the Mexican drag line was a pick, a shovel, and a wheelbarrow. I had to dig a ditch two feet deep and a hundred feet long, in rocky soil. The work was hard and the blisters were many. It was all necessary in order to lay a firm foundation for the building that we were erecting.

Without the proper foundation the building would not stand the test of time.

The Bible has a lot to say about foundations. The word foundation appears in the Bible 84 times. It makes for an interesting study. The following scriptures were used in the writing of this song.

Luke 6:47-49   Whosoever cometh to me, and heareth my sayings, and doeth them, I will show you to whom he is like: He is like a man which built an house, and digged deep, and laid the foundation on a rock: and when the flood arose, the stream beat vehemently upon that house, and could not shake it: for it was founded upon a rock: But he that heareth, and doeth not, is like a man that without a foundation built an house upon the earth; against which the stream did beat vehemently, and immediately it fell; and the ruin of that house was great.

I Corinthians 3:11-15   For other foundation can no man lay than that is layed, which is Jesus Christ. Now if any man build upon this foundation gold, silver, precious stones, wood, hay, stubble; every man's work shall be made manifest: for the day shall declare it, because it shall be revealed by fire; and the fire shall try every man's work of what sort it is. If any man's work abide which he hath built thereupon, he shall receive a reward. If any any man's work shall be burned, he shall suffer loss: but he himself shall be saved; yet so as by fire.

Ephesians 2:19-20   Now therefore we are no more strangers and foreigners, but fellow citizens with the saints and of the household of God; and are built upon the foundation of the apostles and prophets, Jesus Christ himself being the chief cornerstone;

This song is available to stream (just search "Tracy Dartt Foundations of Faith") on Youtube.com

You Are Mine

Sun descended, sky went black,

Shepherd counted sheep

Ninety-nine were safe and sound,

drifting off to sleep

One lamb absent, lost, alone,

shivering with cold

Wondering will I ever find

Master and his fold?

Loving Shepherd leaves behind

slumbering ninety-nine

Lonely lamb be not afraid,

know that you are mine.

Hungry wolves hunt strays at night,

hear their greedy howl

But my Master's tender voice

calls out to me now

Loving Shepherd leaves behind

slumbering ninety-nine

Lonely lamb be not afraid,

know that you are mine

Shepherd carries lonely lamb

back to hundred fold

Master dresses wounds to heal,

now my story's told

Loving Shepherd left behind

slumbering ninety-nine

Calling to this desperate lamb,

know that you are mine

You are mine

Words and Music by Forrest Dartt   Copyright 1996

You Are Mine   Forrest Dartt:

I initially began writing this song as an exercise, just to see if I could tell a whole story in the song without using the word 'the.' It caused me to adjust the sentence structure several times, but it also helped me keep the song very simple. I loved this story since I was a kid, when my parents gave me one of the Arch books called: John and the little lost lamb. Of course, this book made a children's story of the parable of the lost lamb that Jesus told in Luke chapter 15.

I always knew this story was about me. I'm not the type to be following the rules, neatly tucked in with ninety-nine others secure in the fold. I was always the kid that had ventured just a little too far away from the house to be home by dark, and there were many times a police car pulled up beside me and told me sternly: "Get home! Your mother is looking for you!"

Later in life the story took on a new meaning, when I realized the moral that Jesus was illustrating wasn't just about wandering too far from a location. He summed up the point in verse 7, when He said: *"I say unto you, that likewise joy shall be in heaven over one sinner that repenteth, more than over ninety and nine just persons, which need no repentance."* What is repentance? The word repent means to turn away from our sin, and to turn toward God. Modern definitions of the word repent just say 'to feel regret or sincere remorse for one's wrongdoing,' but that doesn't quite express the action that Jesus is talking about. If you are sincere about repentance, you don't just feel really bad about what you did, you will turn away from that path and embrace the righteous way that will lead you home.

Will God forgive you of your sin? Of course He will! He promises in *1 John 1:9, "If we confess our sins, he is faithful and just to forgive us our sins, and to cleanse us from all unrighteousness."*

I've heard many people say things like, "Well the God I worship wouldn't send innocent people to Hell," or "My God wouldn't condemn anyone!" So what is all this business about righteousness and sins and repentance? How can you look in some old religious book and try to apply those old morals to your life now? Well, let me tell you, this is really simple, easy enough for a wayward lamb to break it down for you:

God made you so that He could enjoy a relationship with you.

God loves you and He wants you to love him of your own free will.

We fall short. We can't measure up to the standard of His character.

He knew we could never fix the relationship, so He went ALL IN and did it for us, freely, by sacrificing His own righteous Son in our stead.

All we have to do is believe this in our heart, and confess with our mouth that we accept Jesus as our Lord. Salvation is free and instantaneous. We aren't perfect yet, just forgiven and on the right path, sealed by the Holy Spirit that indwells us within.

Unfortunately, if God going all in for you and making the ultimate sacrifice for you is somehow unacceptable to your way of thinking, then you are choosing to remain unacceptable to Him. There are terrible consequences waiting for those who would deny the voluntary, righteous sacrifice that was made on our behalf, and if it were your son's sacrifice being rejected, you would exact the same sort of penalty without question.

This is the good news, we call it the gospel, found in the Word of God. It means the same thing to all the lost sheep today that it meant back then. The Shepherd is still out there, looking for you, longing to scoop you up so He can return you to the safety and eternal security of His fold. It's time to Lamb up, turn around, and jump into the Master's arms!

Acts 3:19   Repent ye therefore, and be converted, that your sins may be blotted out, when the times of refreshing shall come from the presence of the Lord.

This episode was written by Forrest Dartt

This song is available to stream (Just search "You are mine by Forrest Dartt") on youtube.com

This song is also available for download (just search "Don Dartt You are mine") from the following music subscription services: Amazon Music, Apple Music, iTunes, Spotify, and Youtube Music

Tracy Dartt and Forrest Dartt

First Christmas Day

In a little country town,

In a poor and humble way,

A babe was born in a lowly manger.

It was the first Christmas Day.

There was no shining tree,

No golden gifts to bring.

Just a little band of goodly shepherds

Came to see the newborn king.

And a thousand angels sang, joy and peace to every man.

For God gave His Son as the first gift of Christmas,

That's when it all began.

And a thousand angels sang, till it made the heavens ring.

Glory be to God in the highest, Hallelujah to the King.

Then the child became a man,

And His wisdom all could see.

The Words and the Music and the Tears that Fell

For He brought His message to the people

That all men should be free.

And He taught them peace and love,

And He showed them all the way

To find the gift that God had given

On that first Christmas day.

When a thousand angels sang, joy and peace to every man.

For God gave His Son as the first gift of Christmas,

That's when it all began.

And a thousand angels sang, till it made the heavens ring.

Glory be to God in the highest, Hallelujah to the King.

Glory be to God in the highest, Hallelujah to the King.

Words and Music by Tracy G. Dartt   Copyright 2000

109

First Christmas Day

Do you remember your first Christmas? Well, of course you don't remember the first one, but somewhere in your memory you have pictures in your mind of Christmas when you were a child. For most people those Christmas memories were of pleasant and happy experiences. There was family togetherness, the big Christmas dinner, the Christmas tree, the decorations and the presents. There were community activities and parades.

Where I grew up, in St. Paul, Minnesota, they had a Winter Carnival. There were huge ice sculptures all around town, and an ice palace made of blocks of ice that had been carved out of the nearby Mississippi River. Every year there was a King, a Queen, and a Vulcan, who was the bad guy. The Vulcan had a crew of imps riding on an old fire truck, driving around town, creating mischief. One year a cousin of mine was the Vulcan.

There were many special Christmas activities, but very few that proclaimed the real message of Christmas, the celebration of the birth of Christ, the Savior of the world. There was a lot of emphasis on Frosty the Snowman, Rudolph the Red Nosed Reindeer, and, of course, Santa Claus. Santa Claus is a character who has developed over the centuries from a real person, named Nicholas of Myra, a city in Turkey. He lived from 270 to 243 AD. He was famous for giving gifts to children, as well as to the poor and needy. He was proclaimed a saint by the Catholic church, which is why he is known as Saint Nicholas. He did indeed represent the real spirit of Christmas, the giving of gifts out of a heart of love.

The first gift of Christmas was, of course, God's gift of His only begotten Son, Jesus. The announcement of His birth is recorded in the gospel of Luke.

Luke 2:10-14   And the angel said unto them, Fear not: for, behold, I bring you good tidings of great joy, which shall be to all people. For unto you is born this day in the city of David a Savior, which is Christ the Lord. And this shall be a sign unto you; ye shall find the babe wrapped in swaddling clothes, lying in a manger. And suddenly there was with the angel a multitude of the heavenly host praising God, and saying, Glory to God in the highest, and on earth peace, good will toward men.

Tidings of great joy to all people!! The greatest of all gifts, for in Christ's life, and then in His death, unto us has been given the opportunity to receive the gift of salvation and of eternal life. Have you received the gift of eternal life?

Romans 6:23   For the wages of sin is death; but the gift of God is eternal life, through Jesus Christ our Lord.

This song is available for download (just search "the Dartts first Christmas day") from the following music subscription services: Amazon Music, Apple Music, iTunes, Spotify, and Youtube Music

Tracy Dartt and Forrest Dartt

A Way In A Manger

There was a way in a manger, a way made for me.

For each step from the manger led to Calvary's tree.

And the stars that shone down on the manger that night,

Were the ones that at Calvary in shame hid their light.

So when you sing a song of the Child born that day,

Never forget the Man on the tree.

For the babe Mary placed on that manger of hay,

God made Him the way of salvation for you and for me.

All the world loves to sing of the Child born that day,

But the Man on the cross seems to turn them away.

They sing of peace on the earth, and to all men good will,

But the only real peace is found at Calvary's hill.

So when you sing a song of the Child born that day,

Never forget the Man on the tree.

For the babe Mary placed on that manger of hay,

God made Him the way of salvation for you and for me.

For the dear Son of God Mary placed in that manger,

God made Him the way of salvation for you and for me.

Words and Music by Dan Adkins & Tracy Dartt   Copyright 2000

A Way In A Manger

My Grandson, Taylor, worked for a short time for a company in Nashville called "The Escape Room." It was a couple of rooms with a magnetic door which closed you in until you found the code which opened it. There was a prison break theme, an escape from a broken down space ship theme, being locked into a playground, and several other situations from which to escape. The goal was to find the way out. I didn't try it out myself, but they say that it's an exciting and stressful experience.

In a way, life is like the escape room. We are all born into a world of sin. *Romans 5:12* says this: *"Wherefore, as by one man sin entered into the world, and death by sin; and so death passed upon all men, for that all have sinned:"* "As by one man" (Father Adam), who separated himself from God by his disobedience, all mankind who came after him were born into the world separated from God. Yet our loving Heavenly Father has made a way of escape for us. He made a way of redemption, a way to escape the consequences of man's sin. God sent His only begotten Son into the world, to give His life for the remission, or cancellation of sins.

Many make the fatal mistake of thinking that the accumulation of sins in a person's life is what sends them to Hell. That is not true. Because of Adam's sin, all mankind is under condemnation. All mankind is already on their way to Hell. God is busy rescuing everyone who will receive the gift of eternal life.

Acts 10:43   To Him give all the prophets witness, that through His name whosoever believeth in Him shall receive remission of sins.

Jesus said, *"I am the Way, the Truth, and the Life."* He is the Way! Don't allow yourself to suffer the entrapment and condemnation of sin. Accept the gift that God has given, the gift of eternal life through Jesus Christ.

2 Peter 3:9   The Lord is not slack concerning His promise, as some men count slackness; but is long-suffering to us-ward, not willing that any should perish, but that all should come to repentance.

John 3:15   That whosoever believeth in Him should not perish, but have eternal life.

This song is available for download (just search "The Dartts A way in a manger") from the following music subscription services: Amazon Music, Apple Music, iTunes, Spotify, and Youtube Music.

The Little Gray House With The Clothesline

On a quiet street, in a country town,

Where the children played and the flowers grew 'round,

There a woman lived the days of her life

In the little gray house with the clothesline.

She was just a bride and all her linens were new

When she came to the house with her love so true.

Wasn't much of a cook, but she did laundry just fine

And she hung it out back on the clothesline.

Singing I thank you, Lord, for this beautiful day

And the clean clothes hanging in the sunshine.

Please let your blessings always stay

On the little gray house with the clothesline.

I only met her once, when her baby died,

And I held her hand as she sat and cried,

And we prayed, Oh Lord, send another child soon

To the little gray house with the clothesline.

Well, we moved away but I drove through town

A few years later and when I looked around,

The sight that I saw made me feel so fine,

There were three rows of diapers hanging on the line.

I wanted to stop, but I couldn't stay,

So I said to the Lord as I drove away,

I thank you, Lord, that you heard our prayer

In the little gray house with the clothesline.

Now the years flew by and her child had grown.

She planned a simple wedding with chairs on the lawn.

She tied lilac bouquets on an arbor of pine

And hung white bows on the clothesline.

The Words and the Music and the Tears that Fell

Singing, I thank you, Lord, for this beautiful day,

And the dear ones gathered in the sunshine.

Please let your blessings always stay

On the little gray house with the clothesline.

Well the years were fine, but her skies turned gray,

When the angels came to take her true love away.

But she wasn't alone, friends and neighbors dropped by

To the little gray house with the clothesline.

On an autumn day, as she stood in the wind,

The moment came to see her true love again.

She hung out the towels, but someone else brought them in

To the little gray house with the clothesline.

On a quiet street, in a country town,

Where the children played and the flowers grew 'round,

There a woman lived the days of her life

In the little gray house with the clothesline.

Words and Music by Sharon M. Dartt   Copyright 2013

The Little Gray House With The Clothesline   Sharon Dartt:

In 1972, my husband, Tracy, was asked to travel and sing full-time with Earl and Lily Weatherford and their Gospel group, The Weatherfords. We moved from southern California with our three small children to the little town of Maysville, Oklahoma. The Weatherfords lived in nearby Paoli. Tracy's mother, Virginia, moved with us, and we began a whole new life together. Because Tracy was gone for weeks at a time with The Weatherfords, I visited local churches, and learned of a lady that lived near us. She had just lost her newborn baby. I remember going to visit and sitting next to her and holding her hand as she told me about it. It was her firstborn child, and it seemed to be a case of sudden infant death syndrome, also known as crib death. I tried to comfort her as she wept, then we prayed for the Lord to comfort her heart and to please send another baby soon. I was glad to be with her in her grief, but never saw her again. I never forgot her, though.

Tracy traveled with The Weatherfords for about a year, had a wonderful time ministering in churches and saw more than a thousand salvation decisions in these services. He then made the decision to leave the group and return home to be with his wife and children. We moved into Oklahoma City, and he went to work in a recording studio, helping to produce albums for other artists. In 1974 we moved back to southern California, and in 1976 we found ourselves living in our first tour bus with our children, having sold or given away all of our household belongings. Tracy had begun his solo ministry, singing songs that he wrote himself, and I accompanied him on the piano.

Sometime in the next few years we found ourselves singing in Oklahoma, and decided to drive by the places where we had lived. That's when we saw the rows of diapers on the line, at the house where I had prayed with the grieving mother. What a heart lifting sight!! Something to remember all the rest of my life!!

Several years later, I started to write a song about this experience. The men in the group thought that the title was too silly, and wouldn't even consider listening to the lyrics. Finally, as we were compiling music for a new album in 2013, our son Stoney said, with at sigh, "Okay, let's hear it," and I began to read the words. As I came to the end of the song, Stoney said, wiping tears away, "We've got to get that song on this next album!"

Stoney took the lead on this song, and when he introduced it he would ask, "How many of you have ever hung clothes out on a clothesline?" Most of us use a clothes dryer these days, but I remember the first time we sang this song in our concert. There were only a few in attendance, but afterwards both older couples came up to us and said that the song reminded them of their parents. One lady said that her mother had a baby that died, and her husband added that he had painted her folks house gray for them The other couple said that the song was about their parents, too! I knew then that God was going to bless this song. It had only taken 12 years to get someone to listen to it!!

Ecclesiastes 3:1-4   To every thing there is a season, and a time to every purpose under the heaven: a time to be born, and a time to die; a time to plant, and a time to pluck up that which is planted; A time to kill, and a time to heal; a time to break down, and a time to build up; A time to weep, and a time to laugh; a time to mourn, and a time to dance;

I Samuel 1:20   Wherefore it came to pass, when the time was come about after Hannah had conceived, that she bare a son, and called his name Samuel, saying, Because I have asked him of the LORD.

This song is available for download (just search "the Dartts the little gray house with the clothesline") from the following music subscription services: Amazon Music, Apple Music, iTunes, Spotify, and Youtube Music

Calvary Made The Difference

I know that many men today

are searching, trying to find their way

To happiness and peace of mind.

But like a blind man groping

in the darkness they keep hoping

Some illusive dream they'll find.

But you tell them about Jesus,

And so many won't believe us,

They just turn and walk away.

They say it matters not what god you fear,

As long as you have been sincere,

we'll all reach Heaven some day.

But I say Calvary made the difference.

Jesus proved Himself to me upon the cross.

And He left an empty tomb to remind us He has risen.

And He's Jesus Christ, the only Son of God.

Some men put their trust in drink or pills,

And horoscopes to cure their ills,

But emptiness is all they find.

In their crystal balls and tea leaves,

they find nothing helps or relieves

All the loneliness inside.

But you tell them about Jesus,

And so many won't believe us,

They just turn and walk away.

They say it matters not what god you fear,

As long as you have been sincere,

we'll all reach Heaven some day.

But I say Calvary made the difference.

Jesus proved Himself to me upon the cross.

And He left an empty tomb to remind us He has risen.

And He's Jesus Christ, the only Son of God.

The Words and the Music and the Tears that Fell

Yes, He left an empty tomb to remind us He has risen.

And He's Jesus Christ, the only Son of God.

Words and Music by Tracy G. Dartt   Copyright 2006

Calvary Made The Difference

Acts 4:11-12   This is the stone which was set at naught of you builders, which is become the head of the corner. Neither is there salvation in any other: for there is none other name under heaven given among men, whereby we must be saved.

   My father used to say, "It doesn't matter what you believe, as long as you are sincere." That couldn't be any further from the truth. The religions of the world worship inanimate objects, rocks, volcanoes, trees, statues, etc. Some worship dumb animals and dead ancestors or dead leaders. We met a wonderful Christian missionary at a missions conference in the state of Washington years ago. He was a native man from India and had a moving testimony of how God had turned his life around. He began his testimony with these words, "All my life I served the monkey god." Can you imagine the joy and enlightenment as he learned the truth and accepted the gift of God, salvation through Christ!!

   As Christians, we worship the one true and living God and His only begotten Son, the Lord Jesus Christ. Jesus, our Savior, was crucified, and buried, and by God's glorious power was raised again from the dead. By Christ's death and resurrection, we have the only, ONLY promise of eternal life. Calvary did indeed make the difference.

   My Dad was an alcoholic, and as far as I know, never accepted Christ as his personal Savior. His mom, my Grandma Idie, was an old-time Evangelical Lutheran. She had a great deal of influence on my brother, Don, and some influence on me, as well. When she came to visit, she rode the train from Chicago to St. Paul, Minnesota. We would go down to meet her at the Union Depot, then we walked about a mile together back to our apartment. I always looked forward to her visit. She would always bring me a prize. Once she brought me a little cross that glowed in the dark, and she always had a saying, like "Good, better best, never let it rest, until the good is better and the better is best." Another time she brought me a New Testament. I didn't read it, but kept it like a treasure in my dresser drawer. I hope that Grandma Idie told my Dad about Jesus when he was young. I know that he loved and respected her. I'll keep hoping that Dad is in Heaven, but I won't know until I get there.

I think of Paul's words to Timothy in *2 Timothy 1:5-6; When I call to remembrance the unfeigned faith that is in thee, which dwelt first in thy grandmother, Lois, and thy mother, Eunice; and I am persuaded that in thee also. Wherefore I put thee in remembrance that thou stir up the gift of God, which is in thee by the putting on of hands.*

This song is available for download (just search "BJ Speer Calvary Made The Difference") from the following music subscription services: Amazon Music, Apple Music, iTunes, Spotify, and Youtube Music

Singing Alleluia

I will sing praise to Thee,

I will lift my voice to Heaven.

I will tell of the love,

I will tell of joy You've given.

Singing Allelu, Allelluia

Singing Allelu, Alleluia

Praises to Almighty God,

Creator of the earth and Heavens.

Alpha and Omega, He

Knows the end from the beginning.

Singing Allelu, Allelluia

Singing Allelu, Alleluia

In the beginning was the Word

Tracy Dartt and Forrest Dartt

And the Word was with God,

And the Word was God.

And the Word became flesh and dwelt among us.

And we beheld His glory.

The only begotten of the Father,

Full of grace and truth,

And they called His name

Jesus, they called Him Jesus.

Jesus, they called Him Jesus.

Lord of Lords and King of Kings,

The ruler over all the nations,

I lift my heart in praise to Thee,

Thanking You for my salvation.

Allelu, Alleluia

Singing Alleluia

Words and Music by Tracy G. Dartt   Copyright 1996

Singing Alleluia

Hebrews 13:14-16   For here we have no continuing city, but we seek one to come. By Him therefore let us offer the sacrifice of praise to God continually, that is, the fruit of our lips giving thanks to His name. But to do good and to communicate forget not: for with such sacrifices God is well pleased.

We often use the phrase, "He is worthy of our praise." He is worthy of more than that. The writer of Hebrews says, let us offer the sacrifice of praise. The sacrifice, in the original Greek is thoo-see'-ah which means the act or the victim of the sacrifice, as in the blood sacrifices in the Temple. The significance here is that the sacrifice is total, a life commitment continually. We need to give praise to our Heavenly Father. It pleases Him.

The first recording of this song was made by way of a miracle. I was practicing some new songs that I had written with our church's music minister, when the pastor came through the auditorium and said to me, "Tracy, I'd like to see you in my office." When I got into the office and sat down he said, "Tracy, you need to quit singing with these groups and go out as a soloist. I know you and your testimony, but I don't know the others in your group. I can recommend you to my preacher friends, but I just don't know about the other singers. God is calling you to a new ministry and I want you to pray about it - really pray!" I told him that I would pray about it and talk to my wife about it. I was thinking that Sharon, my wife, would not be open to the idea at all. However, when I talked to her about it, she thought it was a great idea. I couldn't believe her reaction! We prayed about it and we both felt God leading us in that direction.

We had many needs to be met before we were ready to launch across the country. A former business acquaintance offered to buy a bus and lease it to us. Another Christian friend offered to convert the bus to an RV, and quit his job as a barber to do that. He only took three weeks to complete it. He also became our first bus driver and traveled with us for several months. We needed a sound system and our pastor's father donated the money for this.

Another need we had was to record my songs, but I had no money. My publisher, Hal Spencer, told me that if I would bring him a mixed-down tape from a recording studio he would make the record and release it on his label, Manna Music. Soooo......, Lord, how can we pay for a recording?

I was surprised to receive a call from a gospel singer friend, Dean Claiborne. He said, "Tracy, Gloria and I need to record an album, and we want to use your songs and have you produce it for us." I said, "Praise the Lord! I'll produce the recording for nothing, but I want to use the tracks for my own recording." He agreed and it worked out fine because they traveled and ministered in a completely different circle than we did. Thus the Lord provided my first two solo albums. We gave away all of our household possessions and started out on our new adventure with our driver, his dog, and our three young children. Thank you, Lord, for making the way plain for us, and for supplying every need! You've been faithful to provide for us all these years and we praise you for it. Thank you for the years of safe travel and for the hundreds of pastors that opened their churches for us to minister to their people. Thank you for the songs you gave us to share. Thank you for the hundreds of souls saved and for the privilege of being ministers of the gospel. We love you and praise your name!!

This song, and its soundtrack (if you want to use it to perform the song yourself) is available for download (just search "the Dartts Singing Alleluia") from the following music subscription services: Amazon Music, Apple Music, iTunes, Spotify, and Youtube Music

Still The Troubled Waters

Times are hard, but You know that, Lord

Much better than I do.

And I don't know just where I'd be

If it hadn't been for You.

I get confused and it shakes my faith

And I know that shouldn't be.

But sometimes, Lord, I let my worries

Get the best of me.

So, Lord, please still the troubled waters

Calm the storm within me.

Just like You calmed that sea so long ago.

Lord, lead me safely to Soul's Harbor,

Where the waves can rock me gently.

Lord, please still the troubled waters of my soul.

Tracy Dartt and Forrest Dartt

Lord, I know that every puzzle piece

Somehow fits into Your plan.

But it's hard for me to see sometimes,

'Cause I am just a man.

And Lord, I know that when the trial is done

All things work out for the best.

So give me courage and give me strength

And I'll trust You for the rest.

So, Lord, please still the troubled waters

Calm the storm within me.

Just like You calmed that sea so long ago.

Lord, lead me safely to Soul's Harbor,

Where the waves can rock me gently.

Lord, please still the troubled waters of my soul.

Yes, please still the troubled waters of my soul.

Words and Music by Tracy G. Dartt   Copyright 1980

Still The Troubled Waters

Mark 4:39   And He arose, and rebuked the wind, and said unto the sea, Peace, be still. And the wind ceased, and there was a great calm.

Matthew 26:50b-52   Then came they, and laid hands on Jesus, and took Him. And behold one of them which were with Jesus stretched out his hand, and drew his sword, and struck a servant of the high priest's, and smote off his ear. Then said Jesus unto him, Put up again thy sword into his place: for all they that take the sword shall perish with the sword.

Calm the storm within me! Anger is a problem that many people have to deal with. We seem to be living in an angry age. Violence, hatred, murder, protest, conflict and war seem to cover the planet. In our day and time, we are bombarded by so many forms of communication, so many unsolicited opinions, and reports of conflict and anger, that it seems inescapable. As Jesus said, "They that take the sword shall perish with the sword." The Greek word (en) translated simply as "with," has a greater meaning. It signifies to be wholly committed to, in other words, take up the sword in anger and it will consume you. Anger must be dealt with or it will take control of your life.

Jesus said this in *John 14:25-27; These things have I spoken unto you, being yet present with you. But the Comforter, which is the Holy Ghost, whom the Father will send in my name, shall teach you all things and bring all things to your remembrance, whatsoever I have said unto you. Peace I leave with you, my peace I give unto you: not as the world giveth, give I unto you. Let not your heart be troubled, neither let it be afraid.*

Let the peace of the Lord calm the anger within you. The presence of the Comforter, the Holy Spirit, will bring you peace within. Let go of your anger, and take up the cross instead of the sword.

I have learned to get along with just about anyone. There have, however, been a few people that got on my nerves. A few individuals have pressed my anger button. I remember one incident back in my high school days. I walked into the music room for my next class, and for some reason I was angry about something I can't even remember. Roger, a classmate, came into the room behind me. Roger was a really big guy, and had the nasty, irritating habit of coming up behind you and slapping you on the back really hard. Then he would say, "How you doin'?" As I have mentioned, I was already angry, and I reacted by turning around and delivering a punch, hard enough to knock him back over two rows of chairs. The teacher was coming through the room and quickly ducked into his office. It was a "see no evil" moment for him. I heard him whisper "yesss" under his breath as he disappeared. I immediately helped Roger back to his feet and apologized to him. I felt really bad! He wasn't a bad person, he just had some irritating habits. He forgave me and we continued to be friends. I've had a few other incidents in which the Lord gave me the strength to have control over my anger. PEACE BE STILL!!

Ephesians 4:26-27   Be ye angry, and sin not: let not the sun go down upon your wrath: Neither give place to the devil.

This song is available for download (just search "Tracy Dartt Still the troubled waters") from the following music subscription services: Amazon Music, Apple Music, iTunes, Spotify, and Youtube Music

Jesus

If I could live to be a hundred,

If I could see all there is to see,

If I could climb the highest mountain

Or cross the widest sea,

If I could search the whole world over

Much wiser I would be.

But I'd never find one who loves me

Half as much as Thee.

Jesus, Jesus,

Someday I would like to know

Jesus, my Jesus,

How You came to love me so.

They say true love will last forever.

They say true love is very hard to find.

They say true love is sometimes foolish,

Tracy Dartt and Forrest Dartt

And love is sometimes blind.

But You loved me with eyes wide open

And nothing asked of me.

And I'll never find one who loves me

Half as much as Thee.

Jesus, Jesus,

Someday I would like to know

Jesus, my Jesus,

How You came to love me.

Jesus, my Jesus,

How You came to love me so.

Words and Music by Tracy G. Dartt   Copyright 1975

Jesus

Psalms 116:1-4   I love the Lord because He hath heard my voice and my supplications. Because He hath inclined His ear unto me, therefore will I call upon Him as long as I live. The sorrows of death compassed me, and the pains of hell gat hold upon me: I found trouble and sorrow. Then called I upon the name of the Lord; O Lord, I beseech Thee, deliver my soul.

Love holds a place of primary importance in our lives. We need it, we desire it, we find great comfort and satisfaction in being loved, and so does God. The Apostle Paul wrote in *1 Corinthians 13:13, And now abideth faith, hope, charity (love), these three; but the greatest of these is charity (love). It is the very first fruit of the Holy Spirit dwelling within us.*

Have you ever heard that love isn't love until you give it away? Many songs have been written about that saying. It must be understood, however, that love must be received before it can be shared.

John 3:16   For God so loved the world, that He gave His only begotten Son, that whosoever believeth in Him should not perish, but have everlasting life.

John 10:13-15   The hireling fleeth, because he is an hireling, and careth not for the sheep. I am the good shepherd, and know my sheep and am known of mine. As the Father knoweth me, even so know I the Father: and I lay down my life for the sheep.

God so loved that He gave us His Son. Jesus loved so much that He gave His life. The love of God is unconditional. God brings us to Himself with forgiveness. He cleanses us from all unrighteousness, everything that was wrong or ever will be wrong. Our human love is not unconditional towards others. We measure our love out conditionally.

When I was about eight years old, my cousin, Joann would babysit me, while my mother was working. She had a very close friend named Margo. Margo was a very pretty young woman and would come to visit Joann quite often. They were constantly talking about Margo's engagement to a handsome young Marine. They planned and laughed and giggled. Margo was so happy and so very much in love. Then came the day of the wedding. I didn't see it, but I heard about what a beautiful wedding it was. The girls had planned a wonderful honeymoon, spending hours and hours going through brochures and making reservations.

A few days after the wedding, Margo came to visit Joann. She had tears in her eyes. Weeping, she said, "How could he? How could he? It's all over!!" She went on to explain; They had gone to their honeymoon hotel, and when the groom had taken off his shirt, there was a great big, brightly colored tattoo on his chest, with the name of his ex-girlfriend. She said, "I cannot live with that!" Her love was conditional. I can't blame her!

God's love is unconditional!! Praise the Lord!! He forgives and forgets all the marks and scars of our sin. Oh, and by the way, God does have YOUR name etched in the palm of His hand!

Isaiah 49:16   Behold, I have graven thee upon the palms of my hands; thy walls are continually before me.

Psalms 103:10-12   He hath not dealt with us after our sins; nor rewarded us according to our iniquities. For as the heaven is high above the earth, so great is His mercy toward them that fear Him. As far as the east is from the west, so far hath He removed our transgressions from us.

This song is available for download (just search "BJ Speer Jesus") from the following music subscription services: Amazon Music, Apple Music, iTunes, Spotify, and Youtube Music

We'll Be Gone

Many years we all have waited

With our firm position stated,

Looking for our blessed hope, the Lord's return.

On God's Word alone relying,

From the signs there's no denying

That it's soon and very soon, the Lord's return.

And we'll be gone when the trumpet sounds,

We'll be gone when the Savior calls.

We'll be gone away in the twinkling of an eye.

We'll be gone when the work is done,

We'll be gone to our Heavenly home.

We'll be gone to meet with Jesus in the sky.

Now if you've trusted in the Savior,

Keep on trusting, never waver,

'Cause it's coming very soon, the Lord's return.

Tracy Dartt and Forrest Dartt

His Holy Word is never failing,

And you'll suddenly be sailing

As the trumpet sound proclaims the Lord's return.

And we'll be gone when the trumpet sounds,

We'll be gone when the Savior calls.

We'll be gone away in the twinkling of an eye.

We'll be gone when the work is done,

We'll be gone to our Heavenly home.

We'll be gone to meet with Jesus in the sky.

We'll be gone to meet with Jesus in the sky.

Words and Music by Tracy G. Dartt   Copyright 1995

We'll Be Gone

Revelation 4:1   After this I looked, and, behold, a door was opened in Heaven: and the first voice which I heard was as it were a trumpet talking with me; which said, Come up hither, and I will show thee things which must be hereafter.

Over the past many years, we have traveled so much that I find it hard to get excited about a trip anywhere. Alaska, Hawaii, Paris (Texas), nah! I'd rather be home. In the years of travel, we have been in every one of our nation's fifty states, and a few foreign countries. We've seen the Atlantic and Pacific Oceans and the Gulf of Mexico. We've seen the giant redwoods, Yosemite National Park, the Royal Gorge, Yellowstone National Park, Niagara Falls, the Grand Canyon, the Painted Desert, Disneyland, Walt Disney World, and the islands of the Caribbean, just to name a few.

Even our kids would respond with a ho-hum after years on the road, when we tried to point out special places along the way. Finding the letters of the alphabet helped to pass the miles away. The letters J, Q, X, and Z were the hardest. You could always find an X if a highway sign had the word EXIT on it, and Z if you passed a pizza place, but J and Q usually required scanning several dozen license plates as they passed our bus. Our son, Frosty, made up a game for us, called "One Dead Animal." The game began suddenly, when one of us saw a dead animal along the road, and cried out "One dead animal!" The next step was when someone saw two matching items, possibly two fence posts that were close enough together to be seen at the same time. As you may imagine the game got harder as the numbers went up, but if one of us saw another dead animal, they cried out "One dead animal!" and the game started all over again. For the most part, the excitement of travel was past.

I can get excited about Heaven! Jesus promised that He would prepare a place - a REAL place!! After all we have seen of His creation here on earth, we know for sure that the place He is preparing for us is going to be amazing!! And I'm going!! However, I don't know when!!

1 Thessalonians 4:16-18   For the Lord Himself shall descend with a shout, with the voice of the archangel, and with the trump of God:

and the dead in Christ shall rise first: Then we which are alive and remain shall be caught up together with them in the clouds, to meet the Lord in the air: and so shall we ever be with the Lord. Wherefore comfort one another with these words.

1 Corinthians 15:52   In a moment, in the twinkling of an eye at the last trump: for the trumpet shall sound, and the dead shall be raised incorruptible, and we shall be changed.

"In the twinkling of an eye" makes me think of Star Trek - "Beam me up, Scotty." Swoosh!! We'll be gone away. What great joy and comfort to be a born-again believer in Christ, a child of God!! But how sad for the unsaved, the unconverted, who have not received Christ as Savior. Will you be ready for the trumpet sound? Don't be one dead animal!

This song, and its soundtrack (if you want to use it to perform the song yourself) is available for download (just search "The Dartts We'll Be Gone") from the following music subscription services: Amazon Music, Apple Music, iTunes, Spotify, and Youtube Music

What About Me?

A young girl knelt praying, Lord, I want to serve you,

Please won't you use me somehow?

I don't have much money, I don't have much learning,

But I'm giving my life to you now.

For I've heard the preacher telling the folks

How the whole world is lying in need.

Someone should tell them of the sweet love of Jesus,

So I'm asking, Lord, what about me?

What about me? I've known your love,

What about me? I've known Your forgiveness,

And the peace and the joy that Your words

Have brought to my heart.

I'm willing to share if You're willing to use me.

Lord, with this prayer I ask You to choose me.

I know I'm not worthy, but I'm asking You now, Lord,

What about me?

Tracy Dartt and Forrest Dartt

An old man stood praying, Lord, let me serve You.

Please, won't You use me somehow?

For I've spent my whole life to gain earthly treasure

And there's not much time left for me now.

And I know the preacher is telling the truth

About lost folks away cross the sea.

But I've got some neighbors that are bound to miss Heaven,

So I'm asking, Lord,

What about me? I've known your love

What about me? I've known Your forgiveness

And the peace and the joy that Your words

Have brought to my heart.

I'm willing to share if You're willing to use me.

Lord, with this prayer I ask You to choose me.

I know I'm not worthy, but I'm asking You now, Lord

What about me?

The Words and the Music and the Tears that Fell

A young couple stood at the close of a service,

Giving their lives to the Lord.

They soon would be married, and their lives just beginning,

But their hearts had been touched by God's Word.

And as they were standing, the dreams they were planning

For Christ's sake, they gladly deferred.

Neither one knowing that their road would be going

To the uttermost parts of the world.

What about me? I've known your love

What about me? I've known Your forgiveness

And the peace and the joy that Your words

Have brought to my heart.

I'm willing to share if You're willing to use me.

Lord, with this prayer I ask You to choose me.

I know I'm not worthy, but I'm asking You, Lord

What about me?

Words and Music by Sharon & Stone Dartt   Copyright 2000

What About Me?   Sharon Dartt:

I find myself wiping away tears as I listen to this song and type the words. So many memories come flooding back to me. I remember the Sunday night after church when I was 10 years old, and all seven of us kids had gone upstairs to bed. I was one of five girls and two boys at that time, another little brother came along later. I had been in church all of my life, and had heard the Gospel plainly preached many times, but this night I couldn't go to sleep without going back downstairs to tell my Dad that I wanted to pray to be saved. He gladly got down on his knees with me at the dining room chairs, and I cried as I repeated the words he prayed. Just as I thought we were finished, he added, "Help me to mind Mama and Daddy." I somehow knew that this was not the thought of my heart at that moment, and did not repeat it. I just continued crying, and we got to our feet, I knew that God had heard my prayer and saved me.

Years later, my husband, Tracy Dartt, and I, were the young couple that stood at the close of a service on another Sunday night. The preacher had asked if anyone would like to make a commitment of their life, beyond just being a Christian, making their life available to the Lord for whatever He might choose to do with it. Tracy and I both stood to our feet. We knew God had brought our lives together, as we had both been praying for the person God would have us to marry. God saw us standing there that night, and through over 50 years has allowed us to minister with music to his people in churches all over the United States and some other countries. He has given us the privilege of writing and recording songs, teaching for two years in a Christian school, and even giving my husband, Tracy, the honor of pastoring a church in the mountains of California for nearly seven years. We've been able to travel and minister with our four children in seven tour buses, always close together until their college years. What a blessed life we have enjoyed! Looking back on it now, in our 70's, it seems like a wonderful life!! We pray that people will continue to be blessed by the music that God allowed us to create. Only He can make the most of our lives as we commit our lives to Him. He has given every one of us gifts to share. That's just the way He is!! What gift would He want you to share, if you asked Him, "Lord, what about me?"

Romans 12:1-2   I beseech you therefore, brethren, by the mercies of God, that ye present your bodies a living sacrifice, holy, acceptable unto God, which is your reasonable service. And be not conformed to this world: but be ye transformed by the renewing of your mind, that ye may prove what is that good, and acceptable, and perfect, will of God.

John 6:9-12   There is a lad here, which hath five barley loaves, and two small fishes: but what are they among so many? And Jesus said, Make the men sit down. Now there was much grass in the place. So the men sat down, in number about five thousand. And Jesus took the loaves; and when he had given thanks, he distributed to the disciples, and the disciples to them that were set down; and likewise of the fishes as much as they would. When they were filled, he said unto his disciples, Gather up the fragments that remain, that nothing be lost.

This song, and its soundtrack (if you want to use it to perform the song yourself) is available for download (just search "the Dartts What about me") from the following music subscription services: Amazon Music, Apple Music, iTunes, Spotify, and Youtube Music

Born Again Children

Born again children singing a different song

Spreading the word along the way.

Born again children singing a joyful tune

Jesus is coming soon, and this might be the day.

Rising to greet the sun with joy,

Joy comes in the morning.

Thanking the Lord for each new day.

Praising the Lord for all He's done

To bring us salvation.

And spreading the news to all you meet along the way.

Sharing the Gospel.

Born again children, there's been some changes made.

There's never a need to be afraid.

Born again children, life's for eternity.

Jesus has made it free to all who will believe.

The Words and the Music and the Tears that Fell

Rising to greet the sun with joy,

Joy comes in the morning.

Thanking the Lord for each new day.

Praising the Lord for all He's done

To bring us salvation.

And spreading the news to all you meet along the way.

Sharing the Gospel.

Born again children singing a different song

Spreading the word along the way.

Born again children singing a joyful tune,

Jesus is coming soon, and this might be the day.

Born again children, this might be the day.

Words and Music by Tracy G. Dartt   Copyright 1980

Born Again Children

Psalms 96:1-2   O sing unto the Lord a new song: sing unto the Lord, all the earth. Sing unto the Lord, bless His name; show forth His salvation.

A man who attended one of our concerts some time ago came up to me after the program. He was from a country behind the iron curtain. He had been invited to the concert by a friend. He said, "I've never heard music like this before. So much of it is full of joy." He was a new Christian and was thrilled with the music.

Have you ever noticed that much of the world's music is in a minor key? Much of it is sad. Much of our Christian music is in a major key. Many Christian songs are songs of rejoicing, rejoicing in our salvation and the promise of Heaven. We sing a different song as we spread the Word, giving testimony of what Christ has done for us. We are born again children of God, and if we are born again children, we have been changed inside and out. We are new creatures, newly created through the presence of the Holy Spirit dwelling within us.

I played the "church game" for a while in my teens. I attended church, worked on the building, I tithed, even taught a fifth-grade boy's Sunday School class. I had become a religious person, but the real change didn't come into my life until I truly accepted Christ and received the Holy Spirit. The Holy Spirit makes the change in our lives. Once I made a real commitment to the Lord, things changed. My language changed, my habits changed, my attitude changed, and I found that I had a love for people that I did not have before. I was able to forgive, and could even accept myself for who I am in Christ.

Now I was singing a different song. My collection of 1,000 records (45's) I gave away. I found myself listening to different radio stations.

I was hungry for the Word of God. I made new friends and was even bold enough to witness to others. God gave me a loving Christian wife and blessed us with four wonderful children, ten grandchildren, seven great-grandchildren, and the eighth is expected soon. God gave us a wonderful ministry - over fifty years of writing gospel music, singing a different song, and spreading the Word along the way.

John 20:21   Then said Jesus to them again, Peace be unto you: as my Father hath sent me, even so send I you.

Revelation 22:20   He which testifieth these things saith, Surely I come quickly. Amen. Even so, come, Lord Jesus.

This song is available for download (Just search "Tracy Dartt Born Again Children") from the following music subscription services: Amazon Music, Apple Music, Itunes, Spotify, and Youtube Music

First Rays Of Sunlight

Oh, the darkness now is yawning

In the still before the dawning

And the morning soon will break across the sky.

And it seems somehow that hope is gone

For they've crucified the Holy One.

And it seems unfair that He should have to die.

And the shepherds on the mountain mourn,

Who were there the day that He was born.

And the lowly frightened band from Galilee

Sit and wonder what their fate will be,

For He promised them eternity.

But their hopes all seemed to fade at Calvary.

But the darkest hour is just before the dawn,

And the morning's light will soon dispel the gloom.

For now the rising sun tells us that the Son has risen,

As the first rays of sunlight fall upon an empty tomb.

Yes, the darkest hour is just before the dawn,

And the morning's light will soon dispel the gloom.

For now the rising sun tells us that the Son has risen,

As the first rays of sunlight fall upon an empty tomb.

Words and Music by Tracy G. Dartt   Copyright 1976

First Rays of Sunlight

Mark 16:9-11   Now when Jesus was risen early on the first day of the week, He appeared first to Mary Magdalene, out of whom He had cast seven devils. And she went and told them that had been with Him, as they mourned and wept. And they, when they had heard that He was alive and had been seen of her, believed not.

Luke 24:36-37   And as they thus spake, Jesus himself stood in the midst of them, and saith unto them, Peace be unto you. But they were terrified and affrighted and supposed that they had seen a spirit.

You would think that the disciples would jump for joy when the news was brought to them that Jesus had risen from the dead. But, no, they would not believe it. They had to see Him to believe it. Oh, how much we are all like that!

It is said that seeing is believing, but when the disciples saw Jesus standing among them, they couldn't believe that it was true, until He opened their eyes to the scriptures. We always talk about "Doubting Thomas," but they were all doubters at first.

Luke 24:45   Then opened He their understanding, that they might understand the scriptures, and said unto them, Thus it is written, and thus it behooved Christ to suffer, and to rise from the dead the third day:

Those first rays of sunlight must light up all of our hearts, before we can come to believe that the tomb is indeed empty, and that the Lord is indeed risen from the dead. That true light is the Holy Spirit, bringing to us the truth of who Christ is - The Son of God: crucified, buried, and risen from the dead the third day. The disciples found not His body and the angel said that He was alive. It is in the resurrection of Christ that we find the proof of His deity. He is Immanuel, God with us.

In the morning, as the sun rises, the light comes through the windows of our living room. As the sunlight fills our living room, it makes our new day seem alive and fresh. I like to pause and praise the Lord for the sunlight. The sun shines even on a cold winter day. The rising sun brings warmth and life to the grass, the plants, and the trees. The risen Lord has brought light and life to all who believe.

John 1:4   In Him was life; and the life was the light of men.

This song is available for download (just search "Tracy Dartt First rays of sunlight") from the following music subscription services: Amazon Music, Apple Music, iTunes, Spotify, and Youtube Music

Trying To Remember

I said goodnight to my daughter, tucked neatly in bed

my heart was so full of love. The words that I said,

songs that I sang, did not matter as much

as the smile on her face, I reached out to touch

and then it occurred to me, though she had heard me,

she would not remember tomorrow, nor when she has grown

I said goodnight to the Father when the womb was my bed

His voice was so full of love. The words that He said,

songs that He sang, did not matter as much

as the proud smile on His face, the warmth in His touch

as the Heavens He showed me, there were secrets He told me

I cannot remember, nor will I, until I am gone

Oh, Lord, I know how You've known me, and how You still love me

now I'm trying to remember, but it's so hard to see in my mind

Oh, Lord, I have so many questions as I bid you goodnight

from under the moon, and when the sun sheds its light on the day

Please help me remember those moments so tender

I'll try to remember, but will I? Someday I will know...

I will know...

Words and Music by Forrest Dartt   Copyright 1996

Trying To Remember   Forrest Dartt:

Psalm 139:13-18   For thou hast possessed my reins: thou hast covered me in my mother's womb. I will praise thee; for I am fearfully and wonderfully made: marvelous are thy works; and that my soul knoweth right well. My substance was not hid from thee, when I was made in secret, and curiously wrought in the lowest parts of the earth. Thine eyes did see my substance, yet being unperfect; and in thy book all my members were written, which in continuance were fashioned, when as yet there was none of them. How precious also are thy thoughts unto me, O God! how great is the sum of them! If I should count them, they are more in number than the sand: when I awake, I am still with thee.

King David really knew how to express his heartfelt feelings to God, and these verses sparked my imagination, as did the whole chapter, really! When I sang to my infant daughter, I knew she could enjoy my love and attention, but I also knew that she was too young to comprehend what was happening, and she wouldn't be able to remember it later, even though I would. How David was able to conjure this picture in his mind, I will never know, but once the idea was introduced to my mind, it made perfect sense that God would enjoy each one of us the same way we anticipate the birth of our own children. Imagine God personally forming you out of the 'clay' as you developed in your mother's womb! Now imagine as He tweaked your personality, your quirks, your talents, your imagination, your likes and dislikes, and all the things that make you uniquely you! All that intimate detail, down to the color of your hair and eyes, your freckles and other birthmarks, He painstakingly packed it all into the person you are. You are not random! You didn't happen because of science. Your mom and dad were part of the process, but God made you. Personally. On Purpose. Period.

Have you ever felt like you aren't good enough? Of course, we have a sin nature, and we have to be redeemed by the blood of the Lamb, the Lord Jesus Christ, but that isn't what I am referring to at the moment. Do you feel inferior because your body is too large or too small or too plain? Do you wish you were prettier than you are? Do you wish you could sing or dance or draw or paint or play sports or remember numbers or do something or be somebody else? Don't be robbed or fooled into thinking you are less than anyone else. God made you. He fashioned you with great care and detail. He has a vision for what you are to become, and He will ultimately upgrade you with an eternal, perfect body; however, try to remember where you came from, and try to appreciate what you have been given, and use it for God's glory. He has loved you from the very beginning, and it is He who will bring you to the end without any end. And one day, when you stand in His presence, and His spirit whispers a sweet little lullaby that seems so comfortable and familiar, will you remember those moments so tender? We shall see!

This song can be heard on youtube.com, just look up "Try to remember by Forrest Dartt"

Tracy Dartt and Forrest Dartt

Glory Hallelujah

My lips shall praise Thee in the morning

Shall praise Thee with the rising of the sun

For I know that Thou dwellest in the praises of Thy people

And I will praise Thee til the day is done

And I'll sing glory hallelujah

Praise ye the Lord, all ye people

And I'll sing glory hallelujah

For He alone is worthy to be praised

Should I awaken in the midnight

My thoughts shall turn at once to Thee

For Thou hast been my comfort in my time of tribulation

And forever all my praise shall be to Thee

And I'll sing glory hallelujah

Praise ye the Lord, all ye people

And I'll sing glory hallelujah

For He alone is worthy to be praised

Words and Music by Tracy and Sharon Dartt   Copyright 2016

Glory Hallelujah

Revelation 19:1   And after these things I heard a great voice of much people in Heaven, saying, Alleluia; Salvation, and glory, and honour, and power, unto the Lord our God:

In this great passage from the book of Revelation, we see the voices of those who have been saved, set free, and rescued from the curse of sin, and the oppression of the enemy. God's praise is resounding through the halls of Heaven. It will be a wondrous time! We need to be praising God not just in the sweet by and by, but in the nasty now and now! Psalm 22:3 says the Lord dwells in the praises of His people.

1 Timothy 2:1-3   I exhort therefore, that, first of all, supplications, prayers, intercessions, and giving of thanks, be made for all men; For kings, and for all that are in authority; that we may lead a quiet and peaceable life in all godliness and honesty. For this is good and acceptable in the sight of God our Saviour;

We often come to God in prayer with a list of our needs and our wants, but do we stop and take the time to thank Him and praise Him for the things He has already done for us? I love to watch our grandchildren open their Christmas presents. They get so excited that they forget to read the tag or thank the one who gave them the present. Often you ask them the day after who gave them a particular toy, and they cannot remember. Let us remember that every good gift and every perfect gift comes to us from our Heavenly Father. He deserves to receive our thanks and praise!

One of my favorite gospel singers is Amanda Henry from the talented and famous Herb Henry Family out of Modesto, California. Our families have grown very close over the years, and Amanda sang at our son Stoney's funeral. When we are together, Amanda will sing my favorite: "It's the Little Things." It always makes me cry! The song talks about seeing God in all the little things and happenings around us. If you are looking for Him, if you are seeking Him, you will find Him! Take time to notice and appreciate what He is doing for you. You are blessed, and... *All things work together for good for those who love the Lord, and are the called according to His purpose. Romans 8:28*

Study note: the word 'Alleluia' only appears 4 times in the Holy Scriptures, and they are all in the book of Revelation. This tells us that term did not originate here on Earth! It was revealed in John's vision of Heaven and the end of this world. It is a term used in Heaven to praise and worship the Almighty! He has revealed to us that He likes to be praised and addressed in this manner! What a privilege to be provided with the very words God likes to hear us say! Glory Hallelujah, praise ye the Lord all ye people!

This song is available for download (Just search "The Dartts Glory Hallelujah") from the following music subscription services: Amazon Music, Apple Music, Itunes, Spotify, Youtube Music

Born For Paradise

I've been given dominion

in breathtaking gardens of green,

Enjoy pleasant walks with the Master

in the cool of the day

He tells me I'm made in His likeness,

above all the creatures I see

With His gentle touch draws me close,

a smile on His face as He whispers to me

Born into promise, born into light,

Born to a hope that you'll more than survive,

Oh child, you were born for Paradise

Born with a future, perfect design,

Born to inherit the Kingdom divine,

Oh child, you were born for Paradise

Such a shock to the system,

how could He turn me away?

I've broken his trust

by the foolish choices I've made.

I'm bound to a new taskmaster,

to laws locked in tablets of stone.

My mind wanders back to the garden,

back to the day when He told me that I was...

Born into promise, born into light,

Born to a hope that I'll more than survive,

Oh I, I was born for Paradise

Born with a future, perfect design,

Born to inherit the Kingdom divine,

Oh I, I was born for Paradise

Crossing the barrier between us, the Master provides a new way,

And offers the gift of my freedom, my shackles are broken away

The Words and the Music and the Tears that Fell

He brings new life to the promise and I am embraced as a son

His words ring true, love has broken through

Born into promise, born into light,

Born to a hope that I'll more than survive,

Oh I, I was born for Paradise

Born into mercy, born into grace,

Born to recapture the smile on His face

Oh I, I was born for Paradise

Oh I, I was born for Paradise

Oh I, I was born for Paradise

Words and Music by Don Dartt & Mark Townsend   Copyright 2001

Born For Paradise   Don Dartt:

    Anyone who knows me knows that I'm all about film... movies... the making of films, and of making films myself. It's an obsession, and It's been a lifetime pursuit, albeit with my share of life's detours. But those that have known me in more recent years might be

161

surprised to find out I did a stint on the road for most of my 30s, taking a crack at the family biz... writing and singing Christian Music.

My music had more of a contemporary approach than my family's Southern Gospel, but the character, purpose and message were much the same. How could it not? I grew up on a tour bus and my Father's ministry and art form had a profound effect on my life.

In 2001 I released my one and only full length album as a solo artist. I had written or co-written all but one of the songs, but during production my producer friend Mark Townsend and I both agreed we needed one more song to push to radio. I wanted an epic theme, and Mark started by composing the music track.

Here's where my love for film comes back into the story. That previous year I had been obsessed with what is to this day my favorite film of all time, *GLADIATOR,* by Ridley Scott. Mark knew I loved the film's musical score, and his new composition drew inspiration from its timeless themes. As I began to write, I knew the lyric had to be about the journey, about the struggle, about not just survival, but about redemption and victory. This is what formed the spark that became *Born For Paradise.*

Ours is an epic story; how the Creator of the universe formed us in His image with a purpose to not just exist, not just survive, but to THRIVE, and have dominion over His creation. The journey took a major detour with the fall of man. But through the darkest of times, through times under bondage, and "laws locked in tablets of stone" (thanks Dad, for that lyric), the promise endured. That promise is fulfilled in Jesus Christ. Through Him we can once again be embraced as heirs to God's Kingdom, to have closeness with our Creator, and to recapture that smile on His face.

The Words and the Music and the Tears that Fell

Luke 23:42-43   And he said unto Jesus, Lord, remember me when thou comest into thy kingdom. And Jesus said unto him, Verily I say unto thee, Today shalt thou be with me in paradise.

Revelation 2:7   He that hath an ear, let him hear what the Spirit saith unto the churches; To him that overcometh will I give to eat of the tree of life, which is in the midst of the paradise of God.

This song is available for download (Just search "Don Dartt Born for paradise") from the following music subscription services: Amazon Music, Apple Music, Itunes, Spotify, Youtube Music.

Tracy Dartt and Forrest Dartt

I Am A Debtor

I was sorrow, I was sadness, I was tears

I was empty, I was burdened, I was fear

I was alone, I was unloved, I was unkind

I was dead, I was lost, and I was blind

Til I met Jesus and He changed me

He took my life, and He rearranged me

I owed a debt I could not pay

He paid a debt He did not owe

Jesus washed all my sins away

in the crimson flow and now I know

I am a debtor!

Now I am joy, I am laughter, I am release

I fullness, I am freedom, I am peace

I am friendship, I am love, I am light

I am life, I am found, and I am sight

Since I met Jesus and He changed me

He took my life, and He rearranged me

I owed a debt I could not pay

He paid a debt He did not owe

Jesus washed all my sins away

in the crimson flow and now I know

I am a debtor!

Words and Music by Tracy G. Dartt   Copyright 1983

I Am A Debtor

Romans 4:4-5,7   Now to him that worketh is the reward not reckoned of grace, but of debt. But to him that worketh not, but believeth on him that justifieth the ungodly, his faith is counted for righteousness...Blessed are they whose iniquities are forgiven, and whose sins are covered.

I wrote two songs that were inspired by the sermons of Dr. Monroe Parker. This is one of them (The other one was Door of Heaven, covered in a previous episode). Dr. Parker was a fantastic preacher, and a faithful servant of God. He loved the music of the Dartts, and several of our concerts were made possible by his recommendation. I heard Dr. Parker preach the line, "I owed a debt I could not pay, He paid a debt He did not owe," and I immediately knew there had to be a song there!

Our sin debt cannot possibly be eliminated by any amount of good works; It can only be paid for by the shed blood of Jesus on Mount Calvary. *Romans 5:14-15* says: *Nevertheless death reigned from Adam to Moses, even over them that had not sinned after the similitude of Adam's transgression, who is the figure of him that was to come. But not as the offense, so also is the free gift. For if through the offense of one many be dead, much more the grace of God, and the gift by grace, which is by one man, Jesus Christ, hath abounded unto many.*

Father Adam, the first man, committed the first sin. In the Garden of Eden, God told Adam that if he took of the fruit of the Tree of the Knowledge of Good and Evil, Adam would surely die. When Adam ate the fruit anyway, his sin was the sin of disobedience, and disobedience brought on death. Most modern dictionaries define death in a medical sense, but in the good old Noah Webster's Dictionary from 1828, definition number 9 describes death as: "In Theology, perpetual separation from God." Definition number 10 calls it "Separation or alienation of the soul from God, being under the domination of sin and destitute of grace or divine life. Also called spiritual death." OUCH! We inherited this spiritual death from father Adam, but spiritual life comes from knowing Christ. This is why we must be "born again," it is spiritual rebirth when we accept Jesus as Lord.

John 3:5-7   Jesus answered, Verily, verily, I say unto thee, Except a man be born of water and of the Spirit, he cannot enter into the kingdom of God. That which is born of the flesh is flesh; and that which is born of the Spirit is spirit. Marvel not that I said unto thee, Ye must be born again.

I am so glad my debt has been paid! Have you ever been in the drive through, and they told you someone else paid your bill, and you received your order free of charge? That is how Christ took care of our sin debt, and now you are free! Your spiritual life, all of God's Word, His blessings and His promises, an eternal home in Heaven with our Heavenly Father, you are entitled to all of this as a Child of God! Now the only debt we have left is to serve him with thankfulness, praise, and worship. He deserves all of that and so much more because of what He has done for us, and I will gladly forever remain indebted to Him! I am a debtor!

This song is available for download (Just search "BJ Speer I am a debtor") from the following music subscription services: Amazon Music, Apple Music, Itunes, Spotify, Youtube Music

Til The Master Comes Again

Oh, the Son Of Man, He took a far, far journey.

When He left the house He gave each man a job to do.

Oh, He said to work and to watch for His returning

For it may be evening, midnight, morn or noon.

Take ye heed and watch and pray

For ye know not when the time is.

He could come today, all is set for His return.

Take ye heed and watch and pray

Lest He comes and finds you sleeping.

Work and watch and pray 'til the Master comes again.

Lift up your eyes, the fields are white to harvest.

Oh, the work is great but the laborers are few.

God's word to you, my friend, is clearly spoken,

Until He comes there's work for you to do.

So take ye heed and watch and pray

For ye know not when the time is.

He could come today, all is set for His return.

Take ye heed and watch and pray

Lest He comes and finds you sleeping.

Work and watch and pray 'til the Master comes again.

Words and Music by Tracy G. Dartt   Copyright 2007

Til The Master Comes Again

Mark 13:33-37   Take ye heed, watch and pray: for ye know not when the time is. For the Son of Man is as a man taking a far journey, who left his house, and gave authority to his servants, and to every man his work, and commanded the porter to watch. Watch ye therefore: for ye know not when the master of the house cometh, at even, or at midnight, or at the cockcrowing, or in the morning: Lest coming suddenly he find you sleeping. And what I say unto you I say unto all, Watch.

Some years ago, a friend of mine was working for a large corporation in Texas. He had a great job in a manufacturing plant. The plant operated a swing shift schedule, which meant that the workers spent two weeks on morning shift, followed by two weeks on the afternoon shift, and then two weeks of the graveyard shift. My friend had trouble sleeping during the daytime while he was working the graveyard shift. No matter how hard he tried, he could not sleep, and this left him groggy and exhausted.

One night during his shift, he fell asleep while keeping watch on his machine. It just so happened that the foreman came through his area, leading a tour of executive management through the manufacturing floor. Needless to say, my friend was relieved of his duty, and he lost his job as a result of this unfortunate incident. In *Ephesians 5:14-16*, Paul says: *"...Awake thou that sleepest, and arise from the dead, and Christ shall give thee light. See then that ye walk circumspectly, not as fools, but as wise, Redeeming the time, because the days are evil."*

Time is a gift, and it constantly and quickly is slipping away. We need to be about the Master's business, and we must take heed with the time we have been given. God reached out of eternity and created time when He created the light, and separated the light from darkness. Then He called the light "Day," and the darkness He called "Night." This is how He intended for us to mark the passage of time. The evening and the morning were the first day, and God said that it was good.

Time is elusive. We often allow it to slip through our fingers. How many times have you set out to accomplish something, and you thought you had enough time to complete the task at hand, but one thing and then another distracts, delays, or interferes with your plans, and you fail to finish before the allotted time runs out? Our lives are too often busied up with things that don't amount to much in the long run. Of course, we have our jobs, our chores, and the daily tasks and activities that are a necessary part of our daily schedule. But this world is full of distractions that will consume our time and energy on the fluffy stuff of this world, instead of the solid things that have eternal value and bring glory to God. Many of us neglect those spiritual things that are essential to our Christian walk. We need to set time aside for prayer, reading the Word of God, and participating in a local, Bible-believing, church, which is the body of Christ. We need to be prepared for the Master's return. It gets closer every day!

Galatians 4:4-6   But when the fulness of the time was come, God sent forth his Son, made of a woman, made under the law, To redeem them that were under the law, that we might receive the adoption of sons. And because ye are sons, God hath sent forth the Spirit of his Son into your hearts, crying, Abba, Father.

This song, and its soundtrack (if you want to use it to perform the song yourself) is available for download (Just search "Tracy Dartt Til the Master comes again") from the following music subscription services: Amazon Music, Apple Music, Itunes, Spotify, Youtube Music

Tracy Dartt and Forrest Dartt

It's A Nice Place To Visit

This world's a nice place to visit, but I wouldn't want to live here

Wouldn't want to live here eternally

yes, it's a nice place to visit, but I wouldn't want to live here

Jesus is preparing now a better place for me

I've seen this land from coast to coast, from sea to shining sea,

I can't decide what I love the most, it's all so beautiful to me!

I've seen the deserts and the mountains,

the hills and the wide prairie,

But still it doesn't really seem to feel like home to me

This world's a nice place to visit, but I wouldn't want to live here

Wouldn't want to live here eternally

yes, it's a nice place to visit, but I wouldn't want to live here

Jesus is preparing now a better place for me

The Words and the Music and the Tears that Fell

This world's my home away from home, my temporary place

I even know the Builder, how I long to see His face!

He's building me a Heavenly mansion

made of gold and precious stones,

A place to live the likes of which this world has never known

This world's a nice place to visit, but I wouldn't want to live here

Wouldn't want to live here eternally

yes, it's a nice place to visit, but I wouldn't want to live here

Jesus is preparing now a better place for me

Words and Music by Tracy Dartt   Copyright 1997

It's A Nice Place To Visit   Forrest Dartt:

Matthew 16:26   For what is a man profited, if he shall gain the whole world, and lose his own soul? or what shall a man give in exchange for his soul?

1 John 2:15-17   Love not the world, neither the things that are in the world. If any man love the world, the love of the Father is not in him. For all that is in the world, the lust of the flesh, and the lust of

the eyes, and the pride of life, is not of the Father, but is of the world. And the world passeth away, and the lust thereof: but he that doeth the will of God abideth for ever.

I truly had an amazing childhood, living in a bus with my dad as he traveled and sang at churches. We settled down in Sherman, Texas when I was 11 years old, but by that time I had been to the beach on both coasts, been to the Grand Canyon, been to Yellowstone National Park, Niagara Falls, Carlsbad Caverns in New Mexico, Trees of Mystery in northern California, and parts of Canada and Mexico. I went to college in Virginia, and have lived in California, Oklahoma, Texas, and Virginia before finally settling down in Tennessee, which is now my home. When I went in the Army, I visited Germany, France, Spain, the Netherlands, Saudi Arabia, Iraq, and Kuwait, and landed briefly in Rome, Italy, and Cairo, Egypt. I'm not saying any of this to brag on myself, but I want to point out how lovely and diverse and utterly breathtaking each of these places have been at every stop along the way! Most Pastors would take us out to eat at the best restaurant in their respective towns when we visited, some took us fishing nearby, and many gave us a tour of the highlights their locale offered. When my life flashes before my eyes, it's going to be an awesome experience, but I can't wait to see what God has in store for us elsewhere!

What would you do if you won the lottery? Where would you go? What kind of experiences would you cross off your bucket list? Who would you like to meet and spend time with? What is your dream vacation...home...car? Well, guess what? All of the answers as they pertain to this life and this world are temporal, and every bit of it will fade away. *Matthew 6:19-21* says: *"Lay not up for yourselves treasures upon earth, where moth and rust doth corrupt, and where thieves break through and steal: But lay up for yourselves treasures in heaven, where neither moth nor rust doth corrupt, and where thieves do not break through nor steal: For where your treasure is, there will your heart be also."* Christ came to make you the grand prize winner of the spiritual lottery for eternal life! When you give Him your old, sinful heart, He will exchange it for His Holy Spirit indwelling you and sealing your all-expense paid tour of the Heavenlies! There you will meet all the heroes of history and the Bible who gave their hearts to Jesus! Don't pack your things, everything you need will already be there. No return trip is necessary, as it is a one way trip you won't want to, and never have to, return from! See you there!

This song, and it's soundtrack (if you want to use it to perform the song yourself) is available for download (Just search "The Dartts it's a nice place to visit") from the following music subscription services: Amazon Music, Apple Music, iTunes, Spotify, and Youtube Music.

This episode was written by Forrest Dartt

Tracy Dartt and Forrest Dartt

Glad I Decided

I dreamed last night of a faraway place

where the only light shone from God's face

yet it was so bright all the shadows were erased

and I knew that this sight was because of God's grace

and I woke up so excited, I knew it was Heaven

and I am delighted that my sins are forgiven

just knowing I'm invited makes it easier livin'

I'm so glad I decided on Heaven

As I lay back down, all full of cheer

I dreamed of a sound where all I could hear

was the sound of God's praise in my ear

there were smiles all around and the song was sincere

and I woke up so excited, I knew it was Heaven

The Words and the Music and the Tears that Fell

and I am delighted that my sins are forgiven

just knowing I'm invited makes it easier livin'

I'm so glad I decided on Heaven

I'm so glad I decided on Heaven

Words and Music by Forrest Dartt   Copyright 1995

Glad I Decided   Forrest Dartt:

I'm crying as I write this. I can hear my younger brother, Stoney's sweet teenage voice singing along in the background. This is one of the original Dartts' songs from our very first album, the only one I was involved in all the way. Everything was new for us. It was hectic, and there were a lot of unknowns. We didn't have all the money and vehicles and albums we needed when we first started out. It took alot of imagination and a lot of faith, but God provided every single thing we needed when we really needed it (but not when we thought we should have had it, haha!). 23 years later, the Dartts retired from the road.

Now, my little brother, Stoney, is living the reality of this song, and many other songs about Heaven and eternity the Dartts sang over the years. It really is real. It always was, but now it seems closer to me than ever before. I never had a chance to decide whether or not I wanted to be part of this world we live in. I've never completely felt like I fit in here. As soon as I start to feel comfortable where I am and how things are, everything changes. Life gets harder, prices go up, responsibilities multiply, friends and loved ones move on, and even Disneyland gets rid of some of the rides and songs from our favorite old childhood memories and changes them out for something new. Remember the good old days? Well now they are slipping away, and I become more certain with every day that passes that we were never meant to be completely comfortable and fulfilled here. This world is not our final home, we are just passing through.

Heaven is different. Heaven is where I will be able to fellowship with my Maker and my Savior and my Comforter the way it was meant to be in the very beginning. He chose me to be part of His eternal family, and I chose Him. He is preparing me a special place there, and He will receive me unto Himself! *John 14:2-3* says, *In my Father's house are many mansions: if it were not so, I would have told you. I go to prepare a place for you. And if I go and prepare a place for you, I will come again, and receive you unto myself; that where I am, there ye may be also.* My little brother is already there, and that makes it even sweeter. I can't wait to stand beside Him again and sing together! We will sing praises to the King of all Kings who sent his only Son to blaze us a trail so that we could return to Him. He passed through this old world, too. He didn't exactly fit in either, and He certainly didn't settle for the comfort or fulfillment this world could provide! He decided on Heaven for all of us, and it was a much more difficult decision for Him, considering the price He had to pay!

Revelation 21:1-7   And I saw a new heaven and a new earth: for the first heaven and the first earth were passed away; and there was no more sea. And I John saw the holy city, new Jerusalem, coming down from God out of heaven, prepared as a bride adorned for her husband. And I heard a great voice out of heaven saying, Behold, the tabernacle of God is with men, and he will dwell with them, and they shall be his people, and God himself shall be with them, and be their God. And God shall wipe away all tears from their eyes; and there shall be no more death, neither sorrow, nor crying, neither shall there be any more pain: for the former things are passed away. And he that sat upon the throne said, Behold, I make all things new. And he said unto me, Write: for these words are true and faithful. And he said unto me, It is done. I am Alpha and Omega, the beginning and the end. I will give unto him that is athirst of the fountain of the water of life freely. He that overcometh shall inherit all things; and I will be his God, and he shall be my son.

This song, and its soundtrack (if you want to use it to perform the song yourself) is available for download (Just search "The Dartts Glad I decided") from the following music subscription services: Amazon Music, Apple Music, Itunes, Spotify, and Youtube Music

This episode was written by Forrest Dartt

Tracy Dartt and Forrest Dartt

Army Of The Lord

There's an army marching forward,

it's the Army of the Lord

proudly clad in holy armor,

pressing on to their reward

with the Helmet of Salvation,

on their arms the Shield of Faith

and their feet shod with Preparation

of the Gospel of Peace

See the Truth girt round about them,

that through time has stood the test

and their Breastplates brightly shining

with God's own Righteousness

in their hands, they hold a weapon,

'tis a swift, two-edged sword

it's the Sword of the Spirit,

which is the Word of God

The Words and the Music and the Tears that Fell

See they're pressing toward the mark:

the high calling of God

marching forward, claiming victory,

everywhere their feet have trod

listening for that trumpet sounding

to call them to their home on high

to that Hallelujah meeting

in that home beyond the sky

Now they march with jubilation,

loudly now, Hosannas ring!

it's the time of coronation,

they shall crown him King of Kings

and every knee shall bow before Him,

and every tongue confess his name

yesterday, today, forever

never changing, still the same.

now they march with jubilation,

loudly now, Hosannas ring!

it's the time of coronation,

they shall crown him king of kings

and every knee shall bow before him,

and every tongue confess his name

yesterday, today, forever

never changing, still the same

Words and Music by Tracy Dartt   Copyright 1983

Army Of The Lord

Joel 2:11-13   And the Lord shall utter his voice before his army: for his camp is very great: for he is strong that executeth his word: for the day of the Lord is great and very terrible; and who can abide it? Therefore also now, saith the Lord, turn ye even to me with all your heart, and with fasting, and with weeping, and with mourning: And rend your heart, and not your garments, and turn unto the Lord your God: for he is gracious and merciful, slow to anger, and of great kindness, and repenteth him of the evil.

In our day and age, we are seeing an attack against God's people, both Christian, and Jew alike. Even here in the United States, we see an attack against God, against religion, against all Judeo-Christian values and ethics; however, there is a surging movement of Gospel outreach to people who are hungry for and searching for spiritual truth.

As our quartet travelled the United States and Canada, and saw hundreds of salvation decisions, we saw more and more churches beginning to renew their evangelistic zeal afresh. God is still in the salvation business, and he has an army of believers who are unashamed and undeterred from sharing their faith. The Lord is strong, and His Word hits the target every time. *Isaiah 55:11* states: *So shall my word be that goeth forth out of my mouth: it shall not return unto me void, but it shall accomplish that which I please, and it shall prosper in the thing whereto I sent it.*

It is important to remember, we are not an army to attack and defeat unbelievers. We are to win them to the Lord and recruit them to join with us in giving God glory and pursuing the likeness of His Kingdom here on earth. *Ephesians 6:12 For we wrestle not against flesh and blood, but against principalities, against powers, against the rulers of the darkness of this world, against spiritual wickedness in high places.* The evil forces are attempting to thwart the salvation of our fellow men, and our job is to stand in the gap for them, to love them, and to pray for them, even when they are resistant to God's calling. Are you willing to stand in front of the line and advance God's will in your circle of influence? Don't just charge wildly into the fray, make sure you are properly equipped with the armor of God, and have a "battle buddy" who can watch your back. You will need training, prayer, and encouragement, but when you are ready, the Holy Spirit will guide you, protect you, and direct your words and deeds.

Ephesians 6:13-20   Wherefore take unto you the whole armor of God, that ye may be able to withstand in the evil day, and having done all, to stand. Stand therefore, having your loins girt about with truth, and having on the breastplate of righteousness; And your feet shod with the preparation of the gospel of peace; Above all, taking the shield of faith, wherewith ye shall be able to quench all the fiery darts of the wicked. And take the helmet of salvation, and the sword of the Spirit, which is the word of God: Praying always with all prayer and supplication in the Spirit, and watching thereunto with all perseverance and supplication for all saints; And for me, that utterance may be given unto me, that I may open my mouth boldly, to make known the mystery of the gospel, For which I am an ambassador in bonds: that therein I may speak boldly, as I ought to speak.

This song is available for download (Just search "Tracy Dartt Army of the Lord") from the following music subscription services: Amazon Music, Apple Music, Itunes, Spotify, and Youtube Music

Blood Bought Millionaire

I don't have to be an American idol,

or some big superstar

Money and fame and all that I could gain,

never would get me too far

I know my treasures are laid up in heaven

They've been safely stored up there

I don't have to be an American Idol,

I'm a blood bought millionaire

People are going to Hollywood

to try to get their name written in lights

They get busy, forget about God,

and focus on worldly sights

I don't need all this world has to offer

as long as I have Christ

For my name is written in the Lambs Book of life,

by the Creator of life

Tracy Dartt and Forrest Dartt

If I were a celebrity,

it wouldn't get me into heaven for free

If I had the whole world to gain,

it would blind me from the things I should see

One man paid the price long ago,

to clear me of my sin

and by His blood, I have been bought.

That's all I need to win!

I don't have to be an American idol,

or some big superstar

Money and fame and all that I could gain,

never would get me too far

I know my treasures are laid up in heaven

They've been safely stored up there.

I don't have to be an American Idol,

I'm a blood bought millionaire

Words and Music by BJ Speer   Copyright 2005

186

Blood Bought Millionaire   BJ Speer:

I am sure most people can remember the famous hit television show that became a massive success, creating many superstars around the world! I remember watching from the very beginning and choosing my favorite winner each season from this singing competition. I watched each week, and even texted in my vote, as these kids competed for their moment in the spotlight...their chance to be the next big star.

I am so glad that I don't have to compete to be a winner in our music circles. First of all, there is no way I could ever have gone through the nightmare these kids went through just to get to the next level each week. I would have fallen and crashed under all the pressure. Secondly, I already struggle with the judgments and scrutiny of many of the people in our circles, I can't even imagine being under a bigger magnifying glass like they were.

However, I do remember the joy and excitement it brought when I watched... I laughed at the critiques from the judges, as well as gawked at the hard work that was shown from each young person to prove why they should be the next American Idol. The award was a recording contract, and 1 million dollars! That seems like a lot for almost any person. For some, that's all that could be wanted and needed in life. That's what defines you, what makes you who you are. The amazing and more important fact to me, is that each of us are superstars in Gods eyes. We are all winners, and the prize is way more than a million dollars. Our prize, should we choose to accept it, is a lifetime of jewels, mansions, and riches beyond compare. That is so much better than a million dollars. Yes, it is all eternal, but I have won a competition that I didn't even have to compete for. The winning was mine before I started. I didn't have to wait for votes each week, or be critiqued by a panel of people who have nothing better to do. I am a millionaire, bought by His blood, and that's all that's needed for me to win.

I wrote this song in the summer of 2004 to prove that the fame, money and the glory of self is worthless when compared to a lifetime of riches in heaven. I don't need the recognition, or the fortune. But I do hope that with this gift, I can honor and repay my Savior with a lifetime of love, and service to Him. I was a winner before I even started!

Matthew 6:20-21   But lay up for yourselves treasures in heaven, where neither moth nor rust doth corrupt, and where thieves do not break through nor steal: For where your treasure is, there will your heart be also.

This song is available for download (Just search "BJ Speer Blood bought millionare") from the following music subscription services: Amazon Music, Apple Music, Itunes, Spotify, and Youtube Music

Once Upon A Cross

Once upon a time

my life had no reason and no rhyme

Just an emptiness was in this heart of mine

Hopeless, helpless I was lost

'Til once upon a day

someone told me that my sins would wash away

If I'd just believe that God had made the way

once upon a cross

Once upon a hill

the eternal price for sin had all been paid

Once upon a man

all the sins of all the world at once were laid

There God gave his Son

as the sacrifice to pay the awful cost

And gave his life for me,

once upon a cross

Tracy Dartt and Forrest Dartt

Once upon a night

when nothing in the world is going right

And you stumble and you fall without the light

Hopeless, helpless you are lost

Remember once upon a day

someone told you that your sins would wash away

If you just believe that Jesus made the way

to save you once upon a cross

Once upon a hill

the eternal price for sin had all been paid

Once upon a man

all the sins of all the world at once were laid

There God gave His Son

as the sacrifice to pay the awful cost

And gave his life for me,

Once upon a time, once upon a hill, once upon a cross

Words and Music by Tracy Dartt   Copyright 1999

Once Upon A Cross   Forrest Dartt:

Once, it happened one time. Once upon a time is a common line to begin telling a story. A story is a record of what happened. This song documents the experience of someone who had nothing but emptiness until someone told them that their sins would wash away. The real story here is how that fact became possible. God gave His son. Once. He did it one time. When God gave His son, Jesus was separated from all His Heavenly glory. He came to be one of us, to live with us, to love us, and ultimately to accept our penalty of death and separation from God the Father, even though He did no sin and was not required to bear that burden. He was the sacrifice to pay the awful cost. Once.

How many sins can God forgive at once? All of them! When Jesus died on the cross, He fulfilled our penalty once and for all. He forgave all the sins of the past generations who had alienated themselves from God and twisted creation to their evil purposes. He forgave all the sins of His own generation of anger, resentment, hatred, and rebellion by a stiff-necked nation that never seemed to learn their lessons and accept their judgements for their ungodliness and disobedience. He also forgave all the future generations for loving darkness, pleasures, deceit, and loving themselves more than God, truth, justice, and charity. He forgave all my sins, and he will forgive all of yours, too!

The storytelling angle of this song reflects a couple of important things I want to mention. First, the story is telling of actual, historical events that undeniably happened. The life of Jesus, His death upon the cross, and His resurrection, were not only real, they have shaped the entire history of this world around us. The year of our calendar even reflects a relationship to Christ's human existence! The history of America was also shaped by the settlements of people who came to this country to escape religious persecution, and that is how our nation was founded from the beginning. People came here because they wanted to be able to freely worship and serve God.

Second, I would like to remind you that a story is meant to be told. We are to tell the story of Jesus, and what He did for us. If nothing happened in my life or yours, there would be nothing to tell, but we know that is not the case. When Jesus has happened in your life, things changed! Sins were washed away, and that is something that would not have been possible in any other story that did not include the shed blood of our Savior upon the cross. The penalty of eternal separation from God, or death, had been paid for us already. Read the story. Tell the story. Your life is part of the story! Once upon a cross, your sins were washed away. If you have accepted that sacrifice and the free gift of salvation, the story of Jesus is about you, too!

Hebrews 10:12-17   But this man, after he had offered one sacrifice for sins for ever, sat down on the right hand of God; From henceforth expecting till his enemies be made his footstool. For by one offering he hath perfected for ever them that are sanctified. Whereof the Holy Ghost also is a witness to us: for after that he had said before, This is the covenant that I will make with them after those days, saith the Lord, I will put my laws into their hearts, and in their minds will I write them; And their sins and iniquities will I remember no more.

This song, and its soundtrack (if you want to use it to perform the song yourself) is available for download (Just search "The Dartts Once upon a cross") from the following music subscription services: Amazon Music, Apple Music, Itunes, Spotify, and Youtube Music

This episode was written by Forrest Dartt

He Amazes Me

He's there each day when I awake to guide me in each step I take

All the love He has for me just amazes me

When I think He's given all there is of Himself

He surprises me with something else

What He did at Calvary, He would have done it just for me

All the love I see in Him just amazes me

When I think I've got it all and there isn't any more

He gives to me love I never had before

Each night when I thank Him for giving me the day

It's impossible to find the words I'd like to say

The way He has of showing me, the way He always lets me see

All the love He has in Him just amazes me

It's hard for me find simple words to describe

Tracy Dartt and Forrest Dartt

What Jesus means to me, because He constantly

Simply amazes me

Words and Music by Tracy Dartt Copyright 1976

He Amazes Me   Forrest Dartt

My Dad recorded this song on his first solo album, "God's Been Good to Me." I was 5 years old. I loved it when I first heard it, and it is still my favorite song of all after all these years. It is a genuine love song about the Heavenly Father, and I have never heard its equal. It is an unapologetic, intimate, public serenade, without a shred of pretentiousness or self-aggrandizement. From the front pew of the church, I watched my daddy stand up in front of hundreds of people and announce his love for Jesus Christ. Then I followed him and I watched him for a lifetime of backing up those words with his actions.

Tracy Dartt was a humble and kind man. He was a wonderful father, even though he did not have a good example from his own father, who was a crass and violent alcoholic. Jesus took hold on Tracy's life when he was 19 years old, and he never looked back. I never met anyone who loved Jesus more than my dad. He loved the souls of the people around him, and he spent a lifetime of witnessing, singing, and preaching to all of them the good news: that your sins can be forgiven, God has a plan for your life, God will provide all your needs and guide your path if you trust Him, God will never leave you nor forsake you, He is building a mansion in Heaven just for you, and of course, the God on the Mountain is still God when you're down in the valley!

Obviously, I am proud of my Daddy, and I loved him very much, but the real hero of this story is the Lord, God Almighty! He used this humble man to touch the lives of millions. He provided every need our family had every step of the way. He opened doors and inspired songs and provided bushels of souls to be saved. He poured so many blessings on the ministry of the Dartts, we were not able to contain them all, and He is still blessing us after my dad has passed from this life into his Heavenly home.

Thank you, Lord! Praise God! I am so humbled and honored to have been part of the calling and ministry of the Dartts, please bless these words as they go out to your children, and help us all to honor and glorify you with every thought and word and deed and breath. Thank you for the lifetime example of your faithful servant, Tracy Dartt, and help us to carry on the very important work of spreading your good news and your matchless love, grace, mercy, and provision.

Matthew 22:37   Jesus said unto him, Thou shalt love the Lord thy God with all thy heart, and with all thy soul, and with all thy mind.

II Timothy 1:13   Hold fast the form of sound words, which thou hast heard of me, in faith and love which is in Christ Jesus.

This song is available to stream (Just search "Tracy Dartt He Amazes Me") on Youtube.com

This episode was written by Forrest Dartt

Tracy Dartt and Forrest Dartt

He Just Can't Love You Any More

You were so all alone, left to face the unknown

just drifting along with the tide

Tryin' to keep up the pace, putting on a good face

all the while you are hurting inside

Oh, the tears may not show, and the world may not know

but the Father looked down from above

and with grace to impart, from the depths of His heart

He reached out to you in His love

He just can't love you any more, He did all that He could do

He gave Heaven's best, you've been more than blessed

now the rest is up to you

He just can't love you any more, He gave you all that He could give

He did everything to show in your heart of hearts you know

He just can't love you any more

No one else but God's Son could have done what He's done

and no Earthly man ever tried

to give up His throne, and a life of His own

to exchange it for your sin and mine

Oh the blood that He spilt can remove all the guilt

as you call upon Heaven above

and beyond Heaven's gate a home now awaits

secure in the Father's great love

He just can't love you any more, He did all that He could do

He gave Heaven's best, you've been more than blessed

now the rest is up to you

He just can't love you any more, He gave you all that He could give

He did everything to show in your heart of hearts you know

He just can't love you any more

He did everything to show in your heart of hearts you know

He just can't love you any more

Words and Music by Tracy Dartt   Copyright 2007

He Just Can't Love You Any More   Forrest Dartt:

As I have grown older, I have learned more about love and how to love. When I was a child, the greatest love I could understand was 'need' love, needing my parents to provide my needs and show me their affection and attention. In my adolescence, I learned more about admiring others and feeling attracted to someone, introducing the desire to have a deeper, more personal relationship. As an adult, I have learned about marriage and parenthood, about having love that is more about giving than anything else. Most recently, our whole family has learned about losing loved ones, through the passing of my brother, Stone Mountain, and my Dad, the Patriarch of the Dartt family, Tracy Dartt. As much love as I have experienced in my lifetime, it must seem really insignificant to my Creator.

Even when I try to love the Lord my God with all my heart and all my soul and all my mind as Jesus instructed in Matthew 22:37, the love it most resembles is the very earliest 'need' love I had for my parents. You see, even though I have grown and matured and learned more about human love, the truth about my relationship with God is this: His love for me never lessened or grew or changed at all. God's love for me and you has always been turned up all the way to the maximum possible setting! *For God so loved the world, that He gave His Only Begotten Son, that whosoever believeth on Him should not perish, but have everlasting life. John 3:16*

God loved us in our most sinful, rebellious, and fallen state. He gave up all that He had in order to secure our redemption, and He offers all that He has daily as His Word promises provision for all our needs, forgiveness for all we confess, wisdom for those who ask, and an eternal seal for every soul that receives His comforting Holy Spirit. I love Him and thank Him and praise Him for first loving me! Thank you God for your perfect and infinite love, and how experiencing your love helps us to get a tiny glimpse of your great goodness, grace, and mercy as we endeavor to know you better. Help us to emulate your love toward our fellow man, even those who may seem unlovable.

Romans 5:5   And hope maketh not ashamed; because the love of God is shed abroad in our hearts by the Holy Ghost which is given unto us.

This song, and its soundtrack (if you want to use it to perform the song yourself) is available for download (Just search "The Dartts He just can't love you any more") from the following music subscription services: Amazon Music, Apple Music, Itunes, Spotify, and Youtube Music.

This episode was written by Forrest Dartt

Tracy Dartt and Forrest Dartt

The Long Arm Of The Law

I was a child of Adam's fall,

Just a criminal was I.

You've broken one, you've broken all,

No bargain plea, no alibi.

I was running from the law,

There was no place that I could hide.

For the One who made us all

Saw me way down deep inside.

Oh, the long arm of the law

Reaches out for every man,

For no one ever measured up

Since this world of sin began.

But through an act of tender mercy

From the mighty judge of all,

By the loving arms of grace

I was rescued from the long arm of the law.

The Words and the Music and the Tears that Fell

God's perfect standard was too high (for me)

But then the perfect One came down.

He stretched His arms out and He died (for me)

And for my sin grace did abound.

Words and Music by Tracy, Sharon & Stone Dartt   Copyright 2004

The Long Arm Of The Law   Sharon Dartt:

I can't begin to count all the cowboy movies that my husband, Tracy, and I have watched over nearly 58 years of marriage. Stories of bank robberies, cattle rustling, stealing gold or silver mines, and jail breaks were common plots. Unlike real life, the bad guys always got caught by the end of the story, often even killed. But the good guys got hurt, too, and even shot, just like the bad guys. We like to have stories where justice is done. We want to know that the laws will be enforced, and that there will be someone strong enough to bring the offenders to their just punishment. That's the only way we can live in a civilized world.

The real truth is that none of us are without guilt. God created a beautiful garden and made one man and one woman to be in the garden and tend it. There was only one rule - one tree that they were told not to eat of the fruit. When tempted by Satan to doubt the truth of God's warning - if you eat of it you will surely die - the woman ate of the fruit and gave it to her husband. They did not immediately die, but there were surely consequences that were brought upon the entire human race by their disobedience.

The Bible states it this way in *Romans 8:12, "Wherefore, as by one man sin entered into the world, and death by sin; and so death passed upon all men, for that all have sinned:"* But the good news is that God always had a plan, and a Savior was spoken of throughout the thousands of years that followed.

Galatians 4:4   But when the fulness of the time was come, God sent forth His Son, made of a woman, made under the law, To redeem them that were under the law, that we might receive the adoption of sons.

John 3:16   For God so loved the world, that He gave His only begotten Son, that whosoever believeth in Him should not perish, but have everlasting life.

I had the privilege of being one of the Junior Church teachers during the years that my husband pastored in California. Someone showed me a visual illustration that I have never forgotten. Some sins were written in red ink on a white paper, things children may have done. Then a sheet of dark red cellophane was placed over the paper with the words on it. The red words were no longer visible through the red cellophane. This was a picture of how the blood of Jesus, God's Son, covers our sins.

Isaiah 1:18   Come now, and let us reason together, saith the Lord: though your sins be as scarlet, they shall be as white as snow; though they be red like crimson, they shall be as wool.

Thank God for sending His Son, Jesus, to die on the cross, to shed His blood to pay for our sins. We are told in *2 Corinthians 5:20 "For He hath made Him to be sin for us, who knew no sin; that we might be made the righteousness of God in Him."* The penalty for the sins of all mankind has been paid by the blood of Christ. Each one of us can receive the forgiveness of sin and the gift of eternal life by faith in Christ.

So stop running, and turn yourself in. There is no place you can hide from the long arm of the law, but there is no sin that cannot be covered by the blood of the lamb!

This song, and its soundtrack (if you want to use it to perform the song yourself) is available for download (Just search "The Dartts The long arm of the law") from the following music subscription services: Amazon Music, Apple Music, Itunes, Spotify, and Youtube Music

This episode was written by Sharon Dartt

Tracy Dartt and Forrest Dartt

Don't Look Down

Peter and James and John in the boat

and the waves were tossing high.

When the Lord came walking on the water

they began to cry.

Peter said, If it be Thou, Lord,

bid me come to Thee.

Jesus said, Come on,

and Peter stepped out on the sea.

Don't look down at the water,

Peter, just look straight ahead.

If you're looking at the waves around you,

you might lose your head.

Just keep looking ahead to Jesus,

He's your only guide.

When He calms the storm you'll find

you're safe on the other side.

The Words and the Music and the Tears that Fell

Don't look down, don't look down,

Don't look down 'til you're safe on the other side.

Peter walked a step or two,

that's more than you or me.

But looking down into the waves,

the Lord he could not see.

He looked again to Jesus

as he sank into the waves,

Crying out for help because

he knew that Jesus saves.

Don't look down at the water, Peter,

just look straight ahead.

If you're looking at the waves around you,

you might lose your head.

Just keep looking ahead to Jesus,

He's your only guide.

205

When He calms the storm you'll find

you're safe on the other side.

Don't look down, don't look down,

Don't look down 'til you're safe on the other side.

Even though you live for Jesus,

there'll be storms ahead

If you take a step of faith

remember what I've said.

Learn this little lesson from

the pages of God's Word,

Don't let the things around you

take your eyes off of the Lord.

Don't look down at the water, children,

just look straight ahead.

If you're looking at the waves around you,

you might lose your head.

The Words and the Music and the Tears that Fell

Just keep looking ahead to Jesus,

He's your only guide.

When He calms the storm you'll find

you're safe on the other side.

Don't look down, don't look down,

Don't look down 'til you're safe on the other side.

You'll be walking safe and sound,

'long as you're not looking down

Don't look down at the water, children,

just look straight ahead.

If you're looking at the waves around you,

you might lose your head.

Just keep looking ahead to Jesus,

He's your only guide.

When He calms the storm you'll find

you're safe on the other side.

Words and Music by Sharon and Tracy Dartt   Copyright 1996

Don't Look Down   Sharon Dartt:

Matthew 14:26-32   And when the disciples saw him walking on the sea, they were troubled, saying, It is a spirit; and they cried out for fear. But straightway Jesus spake unto them, saying, Be of good cheer; it is I; be not afraid. And Peter answered him and said, Lord, if it be thou, bid me come unto thee on the water. And he said, Come. And when Peter was come down out of the ship, he walked on the water, to go to Jesus. But when he saw the wind boisterous, he was afraid; and beginning to sink, he cried, saying, Lord, save me. And immediately Jesus stretched forth his hand, and caught him, and said unto him, O thou of little faith, wherefore didst thou doubt? And when they were come into the ship, the wind ceased.

When I was a little girl my family lived in Northern California, right on the ocean. We were a large family with five girls and two boys, and I was nine at the time. Our father had a truck that he used to deliver fresh fish to restaurants, hotels, and grocery stores. He would be gone on the fish route for two or three nights of the week, and travel to nearby cities, and even into other states. It was a good job for a dad with all those mouths to feed. We learned to enjoy lots of varieties of seafood, even oysters.

During the summer months, when we were out of school, my Dad would sometimes take one of us older kids on the fish route with him. It was an adventure and we enjoyed the special attention of being with our Dad. However, I vividly remember one very frightening part of the trip, that seemed to happen without warning. My Dad would get sleepy and pull off the road for a short nap. There were times that he would be so close to the edge of a cliff, that I could look right down into the Pacific Ocean far below. Of course, I was by the window on the passenger side, and I remember hardly breathing, and trying not to move, lest the truck should cause the edge of the ground to crumble and we crash into the sea below.

All the while my Dad was peacefully sleeping, I was singing a hymn under my breath. It was "Fear thou not, for I am with thee, I will still thy pilot be. Never mind the tossing billows, take my hand and trust in me." There is much comfort to be found in the hymnbook, and even though there may have been no real danger, I was very much afraid.

The disciples were out on the stormy sea, but they cried out for fear when they saw a figure walking on the water - something they had never seen before. Peter had the boldness to tell Jesus to bid him come, and Jesus said, "Come." We don't know how many steps Peter took before he looked down. We do know that he cried out to the Lord to save him when he began to sink, and Jesus reached out and rescued him.

Have you ever stepped out in faith because you heard Jesus say "Come?" Did you ever look down at all the seeming impossibilities and begin to sink? Do what Peter did - cry out to Jesus. Jesus will not allow you to go under; He will reach down and rescue you and walk with you to safety.

This song, and its soundtrack (if you want to use it to perform the song yourself) is available for download (just search "The Dartts Don't Look Down") from the following music subscription services: Amazon Music, Apple Music, iTunes, Spotify, and Youtube Music.

This episode was written by Sharon Dartt

Tracy Dartt and Forrest Dartt

A Little Bit Of Faith

Old Jonah sorta missed the boat,

got thrown into the deep blue sea

But then he got swallowed by a great big fish,

now, old Jonah was as big as you and me!

Oh, what a fish story, oh glory!

See what a little bit of faith can do

Then there was the prophet Daniel,

got thrown into the lions' den

But an angel of the Lord locked the lions' jaws,

Boy, what a mess that man was in!

It was old Dan who was on the menu,

See what a little bit of faith can do

Joshua and God's army,

they marched around Jericho

On the seventh day the walls gave way.

When they heard them trumpets blow!

The Words and the Music and the Tears that Fell

Oh, what a fanfare filled the air,

See what a little bit of faith can do

A little bit of faith can move a mountain,

a little bit of faith can move a man

It makes something you think you can't do

into something that you can

Just a little bit of faith

Let me tell you about Paul and Silas,

they were singin' in the county jail

When an earthquake made the prison shake,

they didn't even have to post their bail!

Oh, what a jail break, for goodness' sake,

See what a little bit of faith can do

David had to face the giant,

who stood about 9 feet tall

With a rock and a sling David did his thing,

made old Goliath take a fall

Oh, what a knockout without a doubt,

See what a little bit of faith can do

Shadrach, Meshach, Abednego,

got thrown into the fire one day

But an angel of the Lord helped them walk right through,

they didn't even get hot along the way!

Oh, what a bar-b-que, my friend can't you

See what a little bit of faith can do?

A little bit of faith can move a mountain,

a little bit of faith can move a man

It makes something you think you can't do

into something that you can

Just a little bit of faith, I mean a little bit of faith,

a tiny bit. Mustard-seed-sized, yeah!

Words and Music by Tracy Dartt   Copyright 2005

A Little Bit Of Faith   Forrest Dartt:

Hebrews 11:6   But without faith it is impossible to please him: for he that cometh to God must believe that he is, and that he is a rewarder of them that diligently seek him.

Just what does God want from you, anyway? Love? Companionship? Glory? Praise? Worship? Obedience? Yes, God does want all these things from you. But do you know His hot button, His favorite attitude, His number one determining factor for getting radically involved in your life? Faith. That's right, He absolutely digs faith...in Him. Hebrews 11 is an entire chapter that points out many historical heroes of the Bible and their miraculous deeds, and all of it is attributed to the fact that they had faith and acted by faith and God blessed their faith.

So, what is faith? Have you ever heard someone say that so-and-so acted in good faith when they did something? It means they upheld their end of the bargain, expecting that the other party would take care of the rest. Have you ever received a bill, and you slipped your payment into the envelope that says 'no postage necessary' and you sent it? When you put that envelope in the mailbox, you are expecting that the mailman will pick it up, take it to the post office, route it properly, sorting will take place, it will be loaded on the appropriate truck, and it then it will be delivered to the destination you have addressed on the label. The recipient at the other end will remove the check, endorse it, deposit it into their bank account, and credit your customer account the amount of the payment, right? That's quite a lot of expectation to have, but you don't even question it. What a great example of how faith works!

We are not talking about a Genie who grants random, selfish wishes here. We are talking about God instructing you, or laying it on your heart to do something for Him. That is you receiving the bill.

You decide to obey, even though you may not know where the 'payment' is coming from. You write the check. You put it in the envelope that says 'no postage necessary' and you send it back to Him. He will take care of the rest according to your faith.

Does God want you to write bad checks? Absolutely not! So how do you write a check if don't know where the payment is coming from? You write it on God's account. Wait, what??? How do I write a check on God's account? Remember, we aren't asking for something we want from God. We are obeying Him because He is asking something of us. You may ask, does that mean we are paying God back with His own money? Well, yes! Every breath, every thought, every step, every action you take uses resources God has enabled you with. So, when you determine you are going to obey God, serve God, follow God, and worship God, you are doing what He intended for you to do with the resources He gave you. Faith takes just a little extra effort. It requires you to act on the part you can't see yet. Want the waters to part? You must step into the water. Want the Giant to be slain? You must pick up the stone and launch it from your sling. You must stick your neck out far enough that you are really gonna look stupid, or maybe even die, if this thing doesn't work out! You are literally burning your bridges. Again, you had better be sure this is what God wants, and not what you just hope or wish He wants! How will you know? You'll know because you won't really want to do it, but you have no choice because it is the thing that will bring God the glory. God loves you. God loves faith. God does not ignore faith. God wants to reward your faith! God will bless your faith!

How much faith does it take? Not much, but some. Jesus said, "If ye had faith as a grain of mustard seed, ye might say unto this sycamine tree, 'Be thou plucked up by the root, and be thou planted in the sea;' and it should obey you." A mustard seed is very small, but it is measurable, at about 1 to 2 millimeters. There's your answer. It takes a tiny, but measurable amount, of faith to please

God. Do you have enough faith? You aren't supposed to have enough answers to feel comfortable about it, so probably not. It isn't an equation that makes sense when you write it out on paper. You'll never have more than enough. You'll have less than you think you should, and that is probably just the right amount. You want no part of the glory. That's ok, you are right where you should be in this case. Write the check on His account. Seal the envelope. Drop it in the box, and mail it to God!

This song, and its soundtrack (if you want to use it to perform the song yourself) is available for download (Just search "The Dartts A little bit of faith") from the following music subscription services: Amazon Music, Apple Music, Itunes, Spotify, and Youtube Music.

This episode was written by Forrest Dartt

Tracy Dartt and Forrest Dartt

Let Me Be A Rock

The children were a-thirsting in the wilderness,

And Moses cried, Oh, Lord, what shall I do?

Then he heard the voice of God saying, Moses, take your rod,

Strike the rock and waters will come flowing through.

Let me be a rock from which the living waters flow.

Let them grow into a river deep and wide.

Though I may never know everywhere the waters go,

Let the thirsty drink and souls be satisfied.

Let the thirsty drink and souls be satisfied.

Today the souls of men are still a-thirsting

And hearts are crying out to be renewed.

In the desert hot and dry, they will perish and they'll die

Unless the living waters reach them, too.

Let Me Be A Rock

The Words and the Music and the Tears that Fell

Let me be a rock from which the living waters flow.

Let them grow into a river deep and wide.

Though I may never know everywhere the waters go,

Let the thirsty drink and souls be satisfied.

Let the thirsty drink and souls be satisfied.

Let it flow, let it flow to a river, deep and wide.

Though I may never know everywhere the waters go,

Let the thirsty drink and souls be satisfied

Let the thirsty drink and souls be satisfied.

Let me be a rock from which the living waters

Rock from which the living waters flow.

Words and Music by Sharon and Stone Dartt   Copyright 2006

Let Me Be A Rock   Sharon Dartt:

Whenever the Dartts were going to sing this song in concert, I used to introduce it by saying, "Here's Stoney singing, 'Let Me Be a Rock!'" I love songs that come from a Bible story. The book of Exodus, chapter 17, tells us that soon after God delivered the children of Israel out of bondage in Egypt, they came to a place where there was no water for them to drink. The people murmured against Moses, saying that he had brought them up out of Egypt, *"to kill us and our children and our cattle with thirst."* Moses cried unto the Lord, saying, *"What shall I do unto this people? They be almost ready to stone me."* The Lord told Moses to take the elders of Israel, and the same rod he had used when he parted the Red Sea, and to "smite the rock" and water would come out of it for the people to drink. Of course, it happened, just as God said it would. He never deceives us and He never puts us in an impossible situation.

Years later, when the people again needed water to drink, Moses was faced with a similar situation. This time, in Numbers chapter 20, God told Moses to take the rod, gather the assembly and his brother, Aaron, and speak unto the rock before their eyes. Moses gathered the people as God had told him to, but then he disobeyed by smiting the rock twice, instead of speaking to it as God had instructed him to do. The water came out of the rock, but God was displeased with Moses, because Moses relied upon the past experience that he remembered when he smote the rock the first time, instead of obeying the details in God's instructions. Another mistake Moses made was that he asked the people, "Must *WE* fetch you water out of this rock?" His words betray the fact that he thought his own actions were responsible for causing the water to come out of the rock, instead of giving God the glory. It wasn't Moses's miracle to give, it was God's promised provision for His people. As a result of Moses's misobedience, he was not permitted to lead God's people into the promised land.

The words of the song ask: "Let me be a rock from which the living waters flow..." I want God to bring a blessing through my life to those who thirst around me. Will He be able to speak to me in order to make the water come out, or will I be the rock that needs to be struck with the rod? Hopefully, I will obey God's instructions and be a vessel of honor mete for the Master's use as He sees fit. I may never know everywhere the waters flow, but I hope God gets all the glory from it anyway.

John 4:14   But whosoever drinketh of the water that I shall give him shall never thirst; but the water that I shall give him shall be in him a well of water springing up into everlasting life.

This song, and its soundtrack (if you want to use it to perform the song yourself) is available for download (just search "The Dartts Let Me Be a Rock") from the following music subscription services: Amazon Music, Apple Music, iTunes, Spotify, and Youtube Music.

This episode was written by Sharon Dartt

Tracy Dartt and Forrest Dartt

Cool, Clear, Living Water

My thirsting soul within me cried,

a thirst that's only satisfied with water

Cool, Clear, Living Water

My steps had failed, my strength was gone,

I could no longer carry on without water

Cool, Clear, Living Water

but then I read where Jesus said

He helps the thirsting soul that seeks for water

Cool, Clear, Living Water

Like the woman at the well who asked

when she heard Jesus tell of water

once you drink this water in

you'll never have to thirst again for water

I asked and Jesus gave to me springs a-runnin' full and free

and finally my thirsting soul was filled with water

Cool, Clear, Living Water

The Words and the Music and the Tears that Fell

Jesus said come unto me everyone who's thirsty

I'll give you living water for your troubled soul

springing up from deep inside, a well of everlasting life

water of the Spirit to make you whole.

My joyful soul will thirst no more,

I have an everlasting flow of water

Cool, Clear, Living Water

Like the woman at the well who asked

when she heard Jesus tell of water

once you drink this water in

you'll never have to thirst again for water

I asked and Jesus gave to me springs a-runnin' full and free

and finally my thirsting soul was filled with water

Cool, Clear, Living Water

Words and Music by Tracy Dartt   Copyright 1996

Cool, Clear, Living Water

We cannot live without water. Our bodies are made up of 60% water, and our blood is 90% water. We have to have it, or we will be dead in about 3 days. Fortunately, about 71% of the Earth's surface is covered with water. Ancient civilizations and modern cities thrive when they are built along the water. Even salt water can be filtered so that we can drink it. God provided life to the children of Israel by giving them water in the desert, and he saved them from the Egyptian army by bringing His people through the Red Sea, and then crushing the Egyptians by allowing the water to consume them as they attempted to pursue God's chosen. Water is life or death!

The source of our Spiritual existence also springs from the Living Water that Jesus provided us through His Holy Spirit. He told the woman at the well, *"Whosoever drinketh of this water shall thirst again: But whosoever drinketh of the water that I shall give him shall never thirst; but the water that I shall give him shall be in him a well of water springing up into everlasting life. (John 4:13b-14)"* You thirst for that Living Water in your spiritual life, just the same as your body has a need for physical water. Our souls need God. Our inner beings are crying out to Him, and He is the only way to satisfy these needs and longings in your life!

Psalm 63:1-3   O God, thou art my God; early will I seek thee: my soul thirsteth for thee, my flesh longeth for thee in a dry and thirsty land, where no water is; To see thy power and thy glory, so as I have seen thee in the sanctuary. Because thy lovingkindness is better than life, my lips shall praise thee.

Now that you have been blessed with a drink of water from God, will you share with others? You can be a blessing to your fellow man with something as simple as a cup of cold water, and let me assure you, Jesus takes such actions personally! *"For I was an hungred, and ye gave me meat: I was thirsty, and ye gave me drink: I was a stranger, and ye took me in: Naked, and ye clothed me: I was sick, and ye visited me: I was in prison, and ye came unto me...Verily I say unto you, Inasmuch as ye have done it unto one of the least of these my brethren, ye have done it unto me." Matthew 25:35-36, 40b.*

This song, and its soundtrack (if you want to use it to perform the song yourself) is available for download (Just search "The Dartts cool clear living water") from the following music subscription services: Amazon Music, Apple Music, Itunes, Spotify, and Youtube Music

Tracy Dartt and Forrest Dartt

No Greater Love

God looked down upon His creation,

the fulness of time had come

He saw the whole world in need of salvation,

it was time to send down His Son

There must have been a tear in His eye,

as He sent His only Son to die

For you, for me, there is no greater love than this

No greater love than this, no greater sacrifice

To provide us a way to enter His kingdom

with the gift of eternal life

It seems so far beyond what we may understand

There is no other way to explain it, there is no greater love

No greater love than this

Every creature of God's creation

has a need to be wanted and loved

The Words and the Music and the Tears that Fell

longing to be in the arms of the Father

in our Heavenly home up above

So God made a way to redeem you and I

by sending His only Son to die

For you, for me, there is no greater love than this

No greater love than this, no greater sacrifice

To provide us a way to enter His kingdom

with the gift of eternal life

It seems so far beyond what we may understand

There is no other way to explain it, there is no greater love

No greater love than this

Words and Music by Tracy Dartt   Copyright 2016

No Greater Love   Forrest Dartt:

I cannot imagine it. It is unthinkable to me. There are few people that I love enough to imagine risking, possibly sacrificing, my own life for. I know there are others who are willing to risk, and possibly sacrifice, their own lives for the good of the country, or to protect their community. And I suppose it is possible, though you could never be too sure until faced with the situation, that I might consider risking my life at the spur of the moment, such as being caught in the middle of a robbery, a fire, or a terrorist attack, to protect or save someone who is unable to protect themselves, like a small child, or a handicapped or helpless person. But I cannot see any situation in which I would willingly sacrifice any of my children, or choose one to let go of to save one of the others. No way. If you are depending on me to do that for your salvation, you are doomed!

Enter God. He made all of us. He loves all of us. He wants us to be His children, but God cannot stand sin. We are all sinners. I don't mean we were innocently tricked into being sinners, either. We love to sin, and we are good at it. We are rebels by choice. Oh, we are quick to point out and condemn the sins of others, but we jump out of the light when it shines on us. We hide from exposure. We hide our sins from others, and we try to hide from God.

God sacrificed His Son to give us all a chance. Not just the 'good' people, either. God gave everyone a chance by sacrificing Jesus to die on the cross. Rapists, drug dealers, murderers, illegal immigrants, con men, embezzlers, frauds, false prophets, pedophiles, racists, devil worshippers, adulterers, me, and you all have equal access to the cleansing blood of the Lamb, Jesus Christ. The men who crucified Him, those who curse His name, and those who hate everything He stands for are also eligible for His mercy and grace. What makes God able to do this? Why is He not willing that any should perish?

John 3:16   For God so loved the world, that he gave his only begotten Son, that whosoever believeth in him should not perish, but have everlasting life.

II Peter 3:9   The Lord is not slack concerning his promise, as some men count slackness; but is longsuffering to us-ward, not willing that any should perish, but that all should come to repentance.

I am going to be honest with you. I don't deserve it. You don't deserve it. Someone recently pointed out to me that it seems to be giving sinners a loophole, and makes it possible for them to continue to sin even after they have been saved. I answered: Yep. that's true. That's all of us, though. It absolutely is that. We wouldn't stand a chance otherwise. It would be like a flea trying to cross the ocean. Not happening in any way, shape or form. God sending His son to be the sacrifice to offer forgiveness for our sins, the free gift of salvation, and an eternity in Heaven with Him...that was the only way. That's why He was willing to do it. It was the only way!

John 14:6   Jesus saith unto him, I am the way, the truth, and the life: no man cometh unto the Father, but by me.

John 15:13   Greater love hath no man than this, that a man lay down his life for his friends.

Revelation 3:20   Behold, I stand at the door, and knock: if any man hear my voice, and open the door, I will come in to him, and will sup with him, and he with me.

Do you know what else I cannot imagine? I cannot imagine myself, or you, or anyone turning that love away, and rejecting God. Please accept the free gift. Open your door when He knocks on it!

This song is available for download (just search "The Dartts no greater love") from the following music subscription services: Amazon Music, Apple Music, iTunes, Spotify, and Youtube Music. This episode was written by Forrest Dartt

Light Me Now

Fallen into a vicious cycle

can't seem to get back up

Friends pull me down and I'm feelin spiteful

drinking out of a bitter cup

Forgiveness is out of the question

I'll hold a grudge til my dying day

I wish for a chemical reaction

to make reality fade away

I need love, I need a Savior

Someone's got to show me how

I need heroes, not pretenders

Take your candle, light me now

Sometimes I watch you from a distance

You stick out like a swollen thumb

The Words and the Music and the Tears that Fell

Your smile breaks down my resistance

It makes my darkest fears seem dumb

You tell me that you're praying for me

To receive eternal life

You seem to have the answers I need

The truth that pierces like a knife

I need love, I need a Savior

Someone's got to show me how

I need heroes, not pretenders

Take your candle, light me now

You're not perfect, just inspiring

That's the way I feel

Show me by your actions that your

God is really real

I need love, I need a Savior

Tracy Dartt and Forrest Dartt

Someone's got to show me how

I need heroes, not pretenders

Take your candle, light me now

I need love I need a Savior

Take my hand and show me how

I need Jesus, I surrender

Take your candle, light me now

Words and Music by Forrest Dartt   Copyright 2003

Light Me Now   Forrest Dartt:

Matthew 5:14-16   Ye are the light of the world. A city that is set on an hill cannot be hid. Neither do men light a candle, and put it under a bushel, but on a candlestick; and it giveth light unto all that are in the house. Let your light so shine before men, that they may see your good works, and glorify your Father which is in heaven.

Do you ever have that feeling you are being watched! You are! When you are a child of God, you are different from the world around you. You talk differently. You act and react differently. You treat other people around you differently than what they are used to. Your family and friends and neighbors and coworkers are depending on you to be the example of Christ, and your light shines before men. Does that mean you are expected to be perfect all the time? Well, yes, and no. Trust me, they will point out every inconsistency they see in your life that doesn't line up with what they expect from a Christian, so, in a way, they will demand perfection from you. When you mess up in front of them, don't make excuses. Own up to the fact that you are still a work in progress, and make sure they understand you are human, and you don't think more highly of yourself than you ought to. The fact is, we all fall short, and none of us are any better than anyone else. Only the sacrifice of Christ's blood to pay for our sins, the Holy Spirit's seal on our soul, and the righteousness of Christ that God sees us clothed in give us any claim on the Kingdom of God. We didn't earn even a tiny sliver of God's mercy or grace.

Whenever I mess up, and my coworkers remind me what a lousy Christian I am sometimes, I make sure to tell them, "See? I don't have that much of a head start, there is still hope for you as well!" God knows I still need plenty of making over Before I'll be ready to join Him in Heaven. I always try to remember who and what I came from. I want to be a fisher of men for my Savior. I need to love my neighbors and treat them with love and respect. Remember, if you are to be the light of the world, your light needs to shine on the Lord Jesus Christ, not yourself. Your light should benefit others. Your love should benefit others, and in order for that to happen, you have to give it away! Ask God what you need to do to be a blessing to those who are watching you, and ask Him to help you love your neighbors as yourself. You are the light of the world!

Look up The Dartts and Tracy Dartt on most music subscription services to find many of the songs featured in these episodes. You can hear this song on YouTube.com, just search "light me now by Forrest Dartt"

This episode was written by Forrest Dartt

Tracy Dartt and Forrest Dartt

When The Angels Bring Me Home

There's a mansion waiting for me,

just beyond the shores of Glory

Where the ones who've gone before me

wait to bid me, "Welcome home!"

Just beyond the Jordan River

through the pearly gates of splendor

There my Savior will be waiting

when the angels bring me home

Jesus has prepared for me a place to be

on Heaven's blissful shore

A place where sin and fears and pain and tears

are gone forevermore

There's a mansion waiting for me

just beyond the shores of Glory

And I'll have just begun my story

when the angels bring me home

The Words and the Music and the Tears that Fell

I'm looking forward to that city,

just a pilgrim tired and weary

In a strange and far-off country,

waiting for my Heavenly home

Each day my travel brings me closer,

to where I'll see my blessed Savior

He'll say, "Well done," and bid me enter

when the angels bring me home

Jesus has prepared for me a place to be

on Heaven's blissful shore

A place where sin and fears and pain and tears

are gone forevermore

There's a mansion waiting for me

just beyond the shores of Glory

And I'll have just begun my story,

when the angels bring me home

Words and Music by Tracy Dartt   Copyright 1996

When The Angels Bring Me Home   Forrest Dartt:

Mark 13:27   And then shall he send his angels, and shall gather together his elect from the four winds, from the uttermost part of the earth to the uttermost part of heaven.

Luke 16:22   And it came to pass, that the beggar died, and was carried by the angels into Abraham's bosom: the rich man also died, and was buried;

Mankind has always been intrigued by the unknown details of life after death. I am not talking about the parts we have been told. We know that Paul said in *II Corinthians 5:8: "We are confident, I say, and willing rather to be absent from the body, and to be present with the Lord."* But how do we get there? Do we float slowly up above our lifeless body and see a glimpse of everyone in the room? Do we walk from darkness into a bright light? Do we cross the moonlit Jordan river on a log raft steered by a robed, hooded skeleton holding a scythe? I believe there are some things God didn't tell us in the Bible because we aren't supposed to know yet. Some things could be too scary for us to handle with our mortal minds and nerves, but I think it is much more likely that they are mostly things too wonderful for us to know in this life. We like to know stuff. We don't want vague instructions, we want a step-by-step breakdown of every detail in an ordered list.

Let's look at some of the encouraging things we can glean from the scriptures about the moment we leave our mortal bodies. In the verses above, I find great assurance in the fact that **I won't be alone or afraid**. *Psalm 23:4* says, *"Yea, though I walk through the valley of the shadow of death, I will fear no evil: for Thou art with me."*

I have another comforting promise in *Psalm 48:4, "For this God is our God for ever and ever: he will be our guide even unto death."* I am glad to know I will not only have a Companion, but **I will have a Guide**

to help me and show me what to do and how to do it. He has already been through it, and He won't leave me hanging.

God does not ask us to face anything that He was not willing to suffer personally, and **He does not take the experience lightly.** *Psalm 116:15* says *"Precious in the sight of the Lord is the **death** of his saints."*

One more thing I want to note: **Heaven is home!** It isn't some strange, unknown place. Have you ever heard an old, familiar song that made your heart glad, or smelled the smell of a fresh breakfast being cooked and you could almost taste it? Did it bring back a happy memory of a comfortable, secure, space or place in time when and where you belonged? That is what Heaven will be like. When you enter the gate, it won't be like a stranger coming in for the first time, it will be comfortable and familiar. It will be home. There is nothing to fear about going home!

II Corinthians 5:1-5   For we know that if the earthly tent we live in is destroyed, we have a building from God, an eternal house in heaven, not built by human hands. Meanwhile we groan, longing to be clothed instead with our heavenly dwelling, because when we are clothed, we will not be found naked. For while we are in this tent, we groan and are burdened, because we do not wish to be unclothed but to be clothed instead with our heavenly dwelling, so that what is mortal may be swallowed up by life. Now the one who has fashioned us for this very purpose is God, who has given us the Spirit as a deposit, guaranteeing what is to come.

Romans 8:38-39   For I am persuaded, that neither death, nor life, nor angels, nor principalities, nor powers, nor things present, nor things to come, Nor height, nor depth, nor any other creature, shall be able to separate us from the love of God, which is in Christ Jesus our Lord.

Tracy Dartt and Forrest Dartt

Are you prepared to face that moment when the angels come for you? Pray that God will save you from sin and death, and His Holy Spirit will seal your soul unto the Day of Redemption. I'll see you in that Heavenly city one day, when the angels bring us home!

This song, and its soundtrack (if you want to use it to perform the song yourself) is available for download (Just search "The Dartts when the angels bring me home") from the following music subscription services: Amazon Music, Apple Music, Itunes, Spotify, and Youtube Music

This episode was written by Forrest Dartt

The Richest Of Men

If I had gone through my life without a friend to my name

Or a place to lay my head

No family to love me or a friend who cared

Whether I was alive or dead

Then I would still be as rich as the richest of men

With a mansion in Heaven my home

For Jesus my Lord made me heir to His kingdom

And with Him I'm never alone

So I'll just go on my way thanking God for each day

And each promise He's given to me

For He says in His Word He'll supply every need

And He'll guide me where'er I may be

So if you've sought for fortune and the riches of men

Give it up turn away from your sin

Let Jesus my Lord make you heir to His kingdom

And you'll be the richest of men

Yes, you'll be the richest of men

Words and Music by Tracy Dartt   Copyright 1973

The Richest Of Men   Forrest Dartt:

   Bill Gates. George Soros. Jeff Bezos. Elon Musk. Oprah Winfrey. These names represent some of the wealthiest and most successful and influential people on planet earth. They have amassed fortunes so large that there isn't any 'thing' in this world their money cannot buy. With good hard work, savvy investment, an original idea, some startup capital, and a pioneering spirit, plus alot of good luck, you have about 1 in 1,000,000,000 odds of being able to join their company when it comes to monetary value and material things.

   Do you know what else they have in common, that we also have in common? They will not take one penny of their fortunes with them from this world to the next. When we die, we leave it all behind for the vultures to argue about and wrestle over. Death is a result of our sin nature, and that is also something we all have in common. Unless you believe in your heart that God has raised Jesus from the dead, and confess with your mouth that He is your Lord, you will spend that eternal afterlife separated from God, tormented forever in a place called Hell. But even if you do believe, and accept Jesus as your Lord, you still can't take one penny from this world into Heaven.

So what then, does this song mean? What would it mean to be considered one of the richest of men? Where does family, fame, and fortune from this life translate into something eternal? It simply does not factor in, not even one little bit! The only thing you can take with you is what the Holy Spirit can carry, and He cannot touch, nor even associate with, anything unclean or unrighteous. He will carry your soul if it has been cleansed by the blood of Jesus Christ that was sacrificed to wash away the sins of the world, but that is all.

Ephesians 1:12-14   That we should be to the praise of his glory, who first trusted in Christ. In whom ye also trusted, after that ye heard the word of truth, the gospel of your salvation: in whom also after that ye believed, ye were sealed with that holy Spirit of promise, Which is the earnest of our inheritance until the redemption of the purchased possession, unto the praise of his glory.

Job 1:20-22   Then Job arose, and rent his mantle, and shaved his head, and fell down upon the ground, and worshipped, And said, Naked came I out of my mother's womb, and naked shall I return thither: the Lord gave, and the Lord hath taken away; blessed be the name of the Lord. In all this Job sinned not, nor charged God foolishly.

If you are a born-again child of God, then you have the righteousness of Christ draped over you, like a pure, white garment. You have the promise of an eternal home in Heaven, in the presence of God Almighty. You are a part of the Royal family. Don't spend your life with your head hanging down low because of what you don't have down here on Earth. Spend your time and efforts on those things that will be enjoyed for eternity! If you live your life like that, then you can look yourself eye to eye in the mirror and say, "By the grace of God, my Father, I am indeed one of the richest of men!"

1 Peter 2:9   But ye are a chosen generation, a royal priesthood, an holy nation, a peculiar people; that ye should shew forth the praises of him who hath called you out of darkness into his marvellous light;

Matthew 6:19-21   Lay not up for yourselves treasures upon earth, where moth and rust doth corrupt, and where thieves break through and steal: But lay up for yourselves treasures in heaven, where neither moth nor rust doth corrupt, and where thieves do not break through nor steal: For where your treasure is, there will your heart be also.

Look up The Dartts and Tracy Dartt on most music subscription services to find many of the songs featured in these episodes. You can hear this song on YouTube.com, just search "The Richest of Men by Tracy Dartt"

This episode was written by Forrest Dartt

Gloryland

Gloryland, I've never seen it, but I'm going there

I know the builder and I've seen His works before

He's preparing something special just for me

Gloryland, I've heard so much about the things in store

those gates of pearl, and if the streets are made of gold

just imagine what my mansion's gonna be...

Talking 'bout Glory, Gloryland

talking 'bout Glory, Gloryland

I've never seen it, but I believe it

it's not very far they say

if you'd like to see it, better get ready

it's just a heartbeat away

talking 'bout Glory, Gloryland

talking 'bout Glory, Gloryland

Gloryland, Jesus paid the price to take me there

Tracy Dartt and Forrest Dartt

He walked along the dusty road to Calvary

and purchased my salvation on the cross

Gloryland, His resurrection paved the way for me

over death and Hell the victory was made

and He's waiting up in Heaven now for me

Talking 'bout Glory, Gloryland

talking 'bout Glory, Gloryland

I've never seen it, but I believe it

it's not very far they say

if you'd like to see it, better get ready

it's just a heartbeat away

talking 'bout Glory, Gloryland

talking 'bout Glory, Gloryland

Talking 'bout Glory, Gloryland!

Words and Music by Tracy Dartt   Copyright 2007

Gloryland   Forrest Dartt:

This is another song about Heaven, but it isn't just another song about Heaven! It is about the glory of God the Father. He created this Earth and all of its beautiful scenery and creatures to be a reflection of His glory. He even created man in His own image to rule over it all! What a spectacular place, and what a priceless, matchless gift! Unfortunately, we turned away from God's glory. We disobeyed Him because we were told we could be just like Him, and we wanted all the glory for ourselves. The result of our actions resulted in death, an eternal separation from our Creator.

In order to recapture the glory, God had to give us an even better gift, and an eternal life inseparable from His presence! He gave His Son, His innocence, His purity, His righteousness, His justice, and His very Deity. He laid down His life for us as described in the second verse of the song, and the glory was restored forever. There's just one catch: It isn't here on Earth. We have to go through one more separation, we have to let go of our past failure, let go of this cursed place, and let go of the imperfect, temporary vessels we embody in this life so we can partake in the eternal glory of God our Father.

What is glory? It is great beauty or magnificence. Splendor! It is the shine of the golden streets. It is the warmth of His embrace. It is the unified cheer of the saints of God. Honestly, I can't even wrap my mind around it. I don't care that much what it looks like, as long as I can be with my Father. That statement has a double meaning for me now, because my earthly father, Tracy Dartt, is now in Gloryland with my Heavenly Father. I'm going to be honest with you, I can't imagine a sweeter part about Heaven than being with my Daddy! I'd be pleased as punch if it were in a coal mine, but that's not the point.

The point is, Gloryland is everything God has always wanted us to enjoy and experience with Him. Paradise. Utopia! Shangri La!

Gloryland is what men have longed for and dreamed of and hoped to build in this world, but we have always fallen far short. The Tower of Babel, Babylon, Greece, Egypt, Rome, Britain, America, and the European Union! Great ideas, but in the end, we can't do it. Our truest reflection of our greatest glory is a shattered, divided, deceitful, hopeless mess. Our greatest achievement is cell phones, social media and the internet, and our sacred rights to curse and shoot each other. That's the glory of mankind. The reason Heaven is different is because it is a true reflection of the Glory of God. You can't get there without Him. You can't even be you without Him!

Heaven truly is just a heartbeat away. I went to visit my dad in the hospital on the evening of April 6, 2022. He was recovering from a surgical repair to a blockage in one of his intestines a couple of days earlier. Tracy hadn't been able to eat for a week. They tried to turn off his pacemaker so they could do an MRI to locate a loose screw that was in his spine where they had to do surgery some years back because his spine was narrowing and putting pressure on his spinal cord. He was going to dialysis every other day and he had been bound to a either a wheelchair or a hospital bed for most of the last four years. The more I look at this awful paragraph, the more ridiculous it seems to hold this earthly existence so precious! I got off work and went to see Daddy. They were about to pull the tubes out of his throat so he could chew on some ice chips. He was in pain. He was parched. He was suffering. But I prayed with Him that God would make him well.

A few hours later, I was awakened in the middle of the night by a call from my brother, Don. Tracy Dartt had a cardiac arrest. In a heartbeat, he was in Gloryland! God made Tracy Dartt well once and for all! My mom had been listening to this song that very week, and she told me when she heard the mandolins playing on the second verse, it was just like being in Heaven! We played Gloryland at Tracy's funeral as we walked out behind the casket. Glory to God, Tracy Dartt isn't in that box. He isn't in the Ground. He isn't in the

Hospital. He doesn't have a treatment plan, and he doesn't need insurance or social security! He doesn't need his liver or his kidneys to function, because there are no more impurities or waste to remove from his body. Tracy Dartt is in the presence of the Creator of the Universe, the Maker of Man, the Savior of Sinners, and the eternal glory of Gloryland: the God on the Mountain! My earthly daddy wrote that song about my Heavenly Father, and I can't wait to sing it with him in Gloryland!

*1 Chronicles 29:11   Thine, O Lord is the greatness, and the power, and the **glory**, and the victory, and the majesty: for all that is in the heaven and in the earth is thine; thine is the kingdom, O Lord, and thou art exalted as head above all.*

This episode is dedicated to the memory of the life, testimony, and ministry of Tracy Gail Dartt.

January 23, 1944 - April 7, 2022

"...if you'd like to see it, better get ready, it's just a heartbeat away!"

-Gloryland, by Tracy Dartt

This song, and its soundtrack (if you want to use it to perform the song yourself) is available for download (Just search "The Dartts Gloryland") from the following music subscription services: Amazon Music, Apple Music, iTunes, Spotify, and Youtube Music.

This episode was written by Forrest Dartt

He Set It All Aside

Somewhere upon a distant land

long ago and far away

was a crown of gold and precious jewels

still unequaled to this day

a crown desired by kings and princes

throughout the years of time

but the King for who whom the crown was made

for love set His crown aside

So the story goes this King of old

sat upon a throne so bright

glowing like a rainbow in the sky

and around it day and night

those who loved Him paid Him tribute there,

but they all began to cry

when the King for whom the throne was made

for love set His throne aside

The Words and the Music and the Tears that Fell

In that city fair and beautiful,

far beyond the dreams of man

stood a palace of majestic grace

never rivalled, now or then

'twas a place of royal adoration,

but the cheers turned to a cry

when the King for whom it all was made

for love set it all aside

He set aside a golden crown

for a crown of thorns that day

He set aside His Kingly throne

and received a cross of shame

and He traded off the palace grand

for a borrowed tomb, you see

and all He did was all for love,

and the love was all for me

Words and Music by Tracy Dartt   Copyright 1995

He Set It All Aside

Philippians 2:5-11   Let this mind be in you, which was also in Christ Jesus: Who, being in the form of God, thought it not robbery to be equal with God: But made himself of no reputation, and took upon him the form of a servant, and was made in the likeness of men: And being found in fashion as a man, he humbled himself, and became obedient unto death, even the death of the cross. Wherefore God also hath highly exalted him, and given him a name which is above every name: That at the name of Jesus every knee should bow, of things in heaven, and things in earth, and things under the earth; And that every tongue should confess that Jesus Christ is Lord, to the glory of God the Father.

This song was on The Dartts' first album, Now. Our son, Stoney, who was only 17, did a great job on his verse; He had never sung on stage for an audience before, let alone singing a solo. Our album producer was Dan Adkins, a very dear friend of mine who encouraged me to start writing songs again after a long hiatus while I pastored a church in Auberry, California. The band was led by Eddie Crook, who once played Piano for the Happy Goodman family. It was alot of fun going into the studio in Nashville together, and recording our first album as a family quartet. We embarked on a 10 week tour from California to Tennessee in a 15 passenger van that was given to us by a church in Central California the day before we left on the tour. We had one matching suit with 2 neckties each, and a sound system that was loaned to us by a company that wanted us to sell more sound equipment to the churches where we sang. We left it all behind just as if we had good sense, and God blessed us whether we had any or not.

When Jesus left his home in Heaven for a 33 year tour of the middle east, He chose a very uncomfortable location during a particularly tumultuous time of political and religious oppression. He was born in a stable, and laid in a manger used to feed farm animals.

Jesus faced all the same problems and temptations we all do as He grew up and walked this Earth, yet He blessed those around Him with purity, love, truth, healing, and lent His spirit to all those who believed on Him to the glory and fulfillment of His Father's will. He had to suffer a very public humiliation, and a horrific, excruciating, execution for things that He was not guilty of, in order to secure our forgiveness and reconciliation to God. If you ever had any doubt that He loves you, read this paragraph over again. You are the prize that He chose over all the luxury and opulence of the Heavenlies! He wants you to join Him there, and He has taken care of all the obstacles and obligations for you through His death on the cross. Finalize your reservation today, all you must do is believe with your heart and confess with your tongue that Jesus Christ is your Lord and Savior. Do it today!

John 3:15-16   That whosoever believeth in him should not perish, but have eternal life. For God so loved the world, that he gave his only begotten Son, that whosoever believeth in him should not perish, but have everlasting life.

This song, and its soundtrack (if you want to use it to perform the song yourself) is available for download (Just search "The Dartts He set it all aside") from the following music subscription services: Amazon Music, Apple Music, Itunes, Spotify, and Youtube Music

This was the final episode that Tracy worked on with Forrest before he passed away.

Tracy Dartt and Forrest Dartt

Bonus Episode: If You're Not There

I dreamed I went to Heaven,

the end of time had come.

I stood before the Father,

I saw my brand new home.

I greeted all the loved ones,

some friends and neighbors too,

And as I thought back through the years

of all the folks I knew,

You were not there.

While on this earth you wondered

just what would be the price,

And what there was for you to gain

if you should believe.

You watched me from a distance

but never made the choice

To ask God for the new life,

the life that I'd received.

And if you're not there

something will be missing,

Even if I can't recall your name.

The choirs will still sing,

I'll be enjoying everything

That the Lord had meant for us to share.

The jewels in that city

will shine through endless ages,

The Tree of Life provide its fruit so rare.

The golden streets will glimmer,

the living waters flow,

But you will never know if you're not there.

By your will unbending

our friendship could be ending,

Though God had never meant for it to die.

And one soul meant to live forever

but lost in endless night

Will never, ever, ever see that city's blazing light.

Oh, and if you're not there,

something will be missing

Even if I can't recall your name.

The golden streets will glimmer,

the living waters flow,

But you will never know if you're not there.

Maybe I'll forget you, right now I only know

That I will miss you so if you're not there.

Oh, I will miss you so if you're not there.

Words and Music by Sharon & Stone Dartt   Copyright 1999

If You're Not There   Sharon Dartt:

   This song brings much emotion to my heart and mind. I'll probably never know what I was dreaming just before I woke up one morning, a little over 25 years ago, with these four words clearly on my mind. I can't even recall where I was because I was traveling and singing full time with my husband, Tracy, and my son, Stoney. I may have been sleeping in a hotel, in the back of our tour bus, or maybe even in my own bed at home. We had a few days at home sometimes in between trips.

Although I don't know where I was that morning, I surely do know who the song was for. Stoney had met a friend a few years earlier and had done his best to present the plan of salvation to him. The friend, a teenaged boy, had thanked Stoney for explaining it to him. They became good friends and we were pleased to see him when he came to hear us sing at several of our concerts. We always gave an opportunity at the end of our services for folks to make a decision to trust Christ as Savior. Stoney's friend never told us that he had made that decision, even though he knew that the song had been written about him. This friend came to visit Stoney in his room at the Cancer Treatment Center of America in Atlanta in the final month of Stoney's life. They hugged and said goodbye, and Stoney cried as he left. I want so badly to know that Stoney's friend would accept Christ and join us in Heaven one day, but it breaks my heart to know that may never happen. I still pray for him, and I have given him over into the Lord's hands to take care of it.

Is there someone in your life who needs the Lord? Make sure you tell them about the Lord and give them the opportunity to accept Christ. You may be the person God has placed in their life to be a witness. Don't forget to pray for them, that the Holy Spirit will perform His work on their heart and mind to prepare them to be receptive to the gospel message.

Romans 10:8-10, 13   But what saith it? The word is nigh thee, even in thy mouth, and in thy heart: that is, the word of faith, which we preach; That if thou shalt confess with thy mouth the Lord Jesus, and shalt believe in thine heart that God hath raised him from the dead, thou shalt be saved. For with the heart man believeth unto righteousness; and with the mouth confession is made unto salvation...For whosoever shall call upon the name of the Lord shall be saved.

Oh, I will miss you so, if you're not there...

This song, and its soundtrack (if you want to use it to perform the song yourself) is available for download (Just search "The Dartts if you're not there") from the following music subscription services: Amazon Music, Apple Music, Itunes, Spotify, and Youtube Music

<Beep!> See ya, Stoney! - Marty

Thanks and Dedication

There are many people to thank for their help and influence that made this book possible. First of all, I want to dedicate this book to the memory of our Patriarch, **Tracy Gail Dartt**, whose faith, vision, and love for God blazed a trail of Heaven-bound hope for generations to come. I also want to thank my Mama, Sharon Dartt, for her songs and insights in the episodes. She kept the focus on this book and extended the reach of the Dartts' ministry beyond their retirement and the grave. I thank my brothers, Don Dartt and BJ Speer, who contributed songs and episodes and encouragement as well. Mom has said many times that there is nothing more important we could be doing right now. The list of individuals who encouraged and blessed us and prayed for us along the way is too long to list here, but be assured that I am thankful for you, too! Above all, I must thank my loving Lord and Savior, Jesus Christ; my Strength, my Provider, and my Guide, whose miraculous and countless gifts make all things possible…

-The Words and the Music and the Tears that Fell

by Tracy Dartt and Forrest Dartt